WELCOME

To those who lived through it, this was "the war to end all wars". A century of relative European peace following the defeat of Napoleon came to a violent conclusion with the assassination of Franz Ferdinand in June 1914. For four years, vast armies slugged it out across the continent, leaving landscapes scarred, empires shattered and millions dead or wounded.

The war cast a long shadow over the 20th century and it could be argued that we've not yet escaped it today. It's certainly true that this conflict continues to fascinate, inspiring great research, debate and works of art. Here at *BBC History Magazine*, it's a subject we return to regularly and one we'll be covering in significant detail as we get closer to the centenary.

In this special edition, we bring you the story of the First World War, from its bloody inception to its uneasy conclusion. As well as the major battles and personalities, our expert writers also discuss the human dimension to the conflict: what soldiers ate, how they coped with gas attacks, why they visited prostitutes, and how they fared on their return home. I hope that you'll find it a stimulating read.

Rob Attar
Editor

Contents

CONTENTS

IMMEDIATE MEDIA CO

The First World War Story from the makers of *BBC History Magazine* is published by Immediate Media Company Bristol Limited under licence from BBC Worldwide.

BBC History Magazine was established to publish authoritative history, written by leading experts, in an accessible and attractive format. We seek to maintain the high journalistic standards traditionally associated with the BBC.

The First World War Story is produced by *BBC History Magazine*

BBC HISTORY

CONTACT US

WEBSITE
www.historyextra.com

PHONE
Editorial 0117 314 7377
Subscriptions & back issues
0844 844 0250 *Those with impaired hearing can call Minicom 01795 414561*

EMAIL
Editorial historymagazine@historyextra.com
Subscriptions & back issues
bbchistorymag@servicehelpline.co.uk

POST
Editorial *BBC History Magazine*, Immediate Media Company Bristol Limited, Tower House, Fairfax Street, Bristol BS1 3BN, UK

EDITORIAL
Editor Rob Attar
robertattar@historyextra.com
Managing editor Paul McGuinness
Production editor Nige Tassell
Art editor Sheu-Kuie Ho
Picture editor James Cutmore

ADVERTISING & MARKETING
Advertising director Caroline Herbert
Senior advertising manager Laura Gibbs
Account manager Sam Jones 0117 314 8847
Marketing co-ordinator Gemma Burns

PRESS AND PUBLIC RELATIONS
Press officer Carolyn Wray 0117 314 8812
carolyn.wray@immediate.co.uk

SYNDICATION
Head of licensing & syndication Joanna Marshall
Magazine syndication executive Simon Goodman

PRODUCTION
Production director Sarah Powell
Production co-ordinator Emily Mounter
Ad co-ordinator Maria Stanford
Reprographics Tony Hunt and Chris Sutch

IMMEDIATE MEDIA COMPANY
Associate publisher David Musgrove
Publishing director Andy Healy
Managing director Andy Marshall
CEO Tom Bureau
Deputy Chairman Peter Phippen
Chairman Stephen Alexander

BBC WORLDWIDE MAGAZINES UNIT
Managing director Nicholas Brett
Publishing director James Hewes
Editorial director Jenny Potter
Unit co-ordinator Eva Abramik

1914

On the outbreak of the First World War, Europe's borders were significantly defined by its huge empires. The Habsburg Empire of Austria-Hungary dominated the landscape of central Europe, extending from north of Prague right down as far as the southern border of latter-day Bosnia-Herzegovina.

The Russian Empire covered much of what would become Poland. The northern city of St Petersburg had just been renamed as Petrograd, in order to lose the Germanic 'burg' in its name. Meanwhile, the eastern border of Germany reached as far as the Baltic coast of what is present-day Lithuania.

NORWAY

NORTH

SEA

DENMARK

Dublin

UNITED KINGDOM OF GREAT BRITAIN & IRELAND

Hamburg

London

NETHERL.

Brussels

GERMANY

BELGIUM

Paris

LUX.

ATLANTIC

OCEAN

Bay of

Biscay

FRANCE

Munich

SWITZ.

ITALY

PORTUGAL

SPAIN

Madrid

Rome

Lisbon

Europe in 1914

SWEDEN

Petrograd

BALTIC SEA

Copenhagen

Moscow

Danzig

RUSSIAN EMPIRE

Berlin

Warsaw

Kiev

Prague

Vienna

Budapest

Odessa

AUSTRIA-HUNGARY

ROMANIA

BLACK SEA

Belgrade

Bucharest

BULGARIA

SERBIA

MONTENEGRO

Sofia

ALBANIA

Constantinople

GREECE

OTTOMAN

EMPIRE

Athens

MEDITERRANEAN SEA

••• PART ONE •••
THE STORY OF THE WAR

From assassinations to Armistice, **Peter Caddick-Adams** rounds up the 50 key elements that tell the story of the war that was supposed to end all wars

1 THE OUTBREAK OF WAR

Bizarrely, given that 1914-18 was geared to fighting in coalitions, no nation had fully coordinated its military or diplomatic plans with another in the pre-war era. Part of the explanation for the rush to war rests on erroneous assumptions nations made about each other's military capabilities and intentions.

Following the 28 June assassination of the Austrian heir by a Serb, on 5 July Berlin gave Vienna assurances of unlimited support should Austria-Hungary attack Serbia. This assumed Russia was unready for war and would not defend her fellow Slavs, the Serbs. Vienna might have got away with a limited war had she acted promptly, but was late in sending an ultimatum to Serbia, and tardier still in invading.

Eventually, sensing Austro-German mischief, the Tsar ordered Russia's mobilisation as a precaution on 30 July. This, more than anything else, unintentionally lit the fuse, due to the rigid requirements of the Schlieffen Plan (Germany's plan to invade France first, then Russia). Germany had no real reason for war against France at this particular juncture, though her military plans envisaged a Franco-German conflict, but at a time of Berlin's choosing. Now bound to support Austria,

Germany declared war on Russia, and because the very rationale of German General Staff doctrine was to avoid a war on two fronts, began her invasion of France and Belgium immediately, on 4 August. Irrespective of Britain's alliance with France (the Entente Cordiale of 1904) or Russia (signed in 1907), London declared war against Germany at 11pm on 4 August (midnight in Berlin), honouring her treaty obligations dating back to 1839, guaranteeing the neutrality of Belgium.

Germany did not plan for a general war in August 1914, but encouraged it when the opportunity arose. Ironically, the economic indicators are that Germany could have achieved the domination she sought over Europe through industrial strength, had not the war intervened. By contrast, Britain, France and Russia were not keen on conflict that summer, but their foreign policies were not intermeshed sufficiently to prevent it. Though British neutrality in Europe had effectively ended in 1904 with the Entente Cordiale and subsequent military staff talks, no practical dual response to the German threat was devised.

▶▶▶ ARCHDUKE FRANZ FERDINAND – PAGE 18

▲ New recruits march alongside officers at the outbreak of war

GETTY, US LIBRARY OF CONGRESS, ALAMY

2 THE EARLY DAYS: BELGIUM AND SERBIA

Belgium witnessed combat from the first to the last day of conflict, Britain having declared war to defend her neutrality. Belgium's obsolete, 116,000-strong civic guard was unable to halt the Germans, and most of the country soon fell under German domination. By November 1914, only the Ypres salient remained in Allied hands – hence the determination to retain the last portion of sovereign Belgian territory.

During the war, under the command of King Albert I, the Belgian army held the low-lying sector between Ypres and Nieuwpoort on the coast, but did not participate in any of the major Allied offensives until the last month of the war. By 1918, it had grown to 166,000 men, forming one cavalry and twelve infantry divisions, and its air force grew to about 200 useful machines. Yet the war cost Belgium more than 14,000 military dead and 44,686 wounded.

The opening shots that triggered the war were fired on 28 June 1914 by a Bosnian-

Serb, killing the Austrian heir. Following the assassination of Archduke Franz Ferdinand in Sarajevo, Austria blamed Serbia for inciting violence and declared war. The first Austro-Hungarian attackers massacred civilians before the 420,000-strong Serbian army drove them back across their border a week later – the first Allied victory of the war.

Typhus had so weakened the Serbians in 1915 that when the Austrians attacked in October, the army was obliged to retreat, abandoning Belgrade on the 9th. Two days later, Bulgaria declared war, intending to annex the Serb possession of Macedonia. The Serbian army fought well but, perilously low on ammunition, withdrew with 200,000 soldiers and civilians over snow-covered mountains into Albania, where it was to be evacuated by sea to Corfu. The trek cost the lives of 20,000.

On 29 September 1918, Bulgaria surrendered, whereupon French, British and Serbian troops (re-equipped and

▲ Dead horses litter the road following the August 1914 Battle of Haelen in Belgium

trained by the Allies) drove all remaining Austro-German forces out of Serbia. Military casualties, at 320,000 wounded and dead from combat or illness, were greatly exceeded by civilian deaths - nearly 650,000. The majority of these were due to typhus and famine, rather than combat.

3 THE FRUSTRATIONS OF THE FRENCH ARMY

In 1914, every Frenchman aged 20 was liable for conscription, serving for two years with the Regulars, then eleven in the Reserve, when they could be recalled for refresher courses from their civilian jobs. They concluded with 15 years in the territorial army (in French, *les pépères*, the grandads).

From 1 August 1914, France mobilised her 800,000 regulars and 2.9 million trained reserves and territorials. Mobilisation was slick and support for the war was high. The doctrine was simple: according

to Field Service Regulations, 1913, 'The French army, returning to its traditions, recognises no law save that of the offensive'.

French defensive strategy followed Plan XVII – an offensive into Alsace-Lorraine, a move the Germans had predicted and sought to outflank using the Schlieffen Plan. But, within a few weeks, the French were back in their starting positions, having lost over 300,000 men.

For the next 18 months the French commander, Joffre, mounted repeated offensives, which produced

mounting casualties. Verdun accelerated these losses and, by the end of 1916, the army had suffered 860,000 fatalities since 1914. Men were conscripted up to the age of 45, and trench newspapers testify to the plight of soldiers who endured harsh conditions, monotonous food and irregular leave.

The failure of Robert Nivelle's 16 April 1917 offensive on the Chemin des Dames stirred deep-seated discontent into open mutiny. Some 49 out of 113 divisions were affected by unrest. Soldiers simply refused to go to the front. This was not revolution but the response of citizen soldiers to intolerable conditions. Pétain, who succeeded him, restored morale by a judicious mixture of firmness (nearly 3,500 courts martial and 50 executions) and attention to his troops' demands.

On 26 March 1918, Ferdinand Foch was appointed supreme Allied commander, leading his army to victory, but French losses would be catastrophic: 8,317,000 men, including 475,000 colonial troops, were conscripted, of whom 4.2 million became casualties, including 1.3 million dead.

◄ The French army mobilises following the German declaration of war on Russia, 1914

4 THE RISE AND FALL OF THE GERMAN ARMY

The Kaiserheer (Imperial Army) that fought the First World War, though building on earlier traditions, dated from the 1871 German unification. It combined about 500,000 conscript regulars from the Prussian, Bavarian, Saxon and Württemberg royal forces, plus reservists. From 17 years old, men were liable for successive service in the Active, Reserve, Landwehr and Landsturm forces, or the supplementary reserve (Ersatz), until the age of 45.

Germany's army changed radically during the war, especially under Hindenburg and Ludendorff, appointed in 1916. They became effective dictators of the war effort, mobilising the state for total war. Manpower and resource shortages forced innovative tactical doctrine. The result was a move from linear trenches to 'elastic' defence in depth, based on strong-points and counterattack units. Over the winter of 1916-17 the Siegfried Stellung (Hindenburg Line) was constructed in the west using these principles, and in February 1917 they fell back to this new position.

Offensive doctrine included stormtroops (sturmtruppen), developed by Hauptmann Willy Rohr and implemented by junior commanders like Erwin Rommel and Ernst Jünger during 1916-17. Superbly-trained small shock units used for infiltration, they were an efficient alternative to large frontal attacks, which attracted heavy casualties. They were accompanied by the radical 'hurricane' artillery methods of commander Georg Bruchmüller. Germany's 21 March 1918 offensive incorporated many of these techniques, but with few tanks or cavalry, it had no means of exploitation, and divisions found themselves at the end of overstretched communication lines, exhausted.

They were easy prey for the Allied counter-offensive, which started at Amiens on 8 August. From then until the Armistice, the Germans were forced back, having lost the initiative. Although their officer corps tried to evade blame for their defeat, the German army was decisively beaten in the field. Sources vary, but 11 million appear to have been mobilised, of whom over 4.1 million were wounded and 1.7 million killed.

US LIBRARY OF CONGRESS X3

▼ The German army suffered millions of casualties in ultimate defeat

5 THE DYING DAYS OF THE AUSTRO-HUNGARIAN EMPIRE

The Habsburg monarchs reigned simultaneously as Emperors of Austria and Kings of Hungary, with a kingdom that included modern-day Bosnia-Herzegovina, Croatia, the Czech Republic, Slovakia, Slovenia, much of Serbia and Romania, and parts of Italy, Montenegro, Poland and Ukraine. Allegedly, Hungary gave the resources and men, while Austria provided the leadership. Its unwieldy army was officered by Austrians, contained Slav, Hungarian, Romanian and Italian conscripts (often with their own nationalist agendas) who responded to three languages of command – German, Magyar and Serbo-Croat.

By 1914, it had become obvious to many that the regime would not be able to survive the various calls for independence from her multinational citizens. The Slavs in the ranks created problems when they refused to fight against their Russian brethren. When an Austro-German force attacked Italy in 1917, Erich Ludendorff noted in his post-war memoirs that "the attack on Italy was necessary in order to prevent the collapse of Austria-Hungary".

Having started the war with inadequate weapons and equipment, Austrian military capability was always compromised by poor logistics and a lack of pre-war military spending and procurement. Her high command had no plans for waging continental war, assuming that any future conflict would be a regional, Balkan one. In this sense, Austria-Hungary was mismatched with Germany, who out-spent most countries on armaments and planned for large-scale war.

The empire's military track record was poor: in 1914, the army attacked Serbia, but lost over half of its 450,000 men. On the Eastern Front, it generally did well when operating under German command, due to the sheer ineptitude of Russia's leadership and the poverty of her equipment. But it came at a cost of one million casualties. In Italy, under German tutelage, Austria proved effective, managing to hold back the numerically superior Italian armies along the Isonzo and forging ahead at Caporetto (again with German help) in 1917. Although Austria generally welcomed the Kaiser's intervention, Germany came to believe that with the alliance, she was "shackled to a corpse".

▲ An Austrian officer awaits treatment. Did Austria provide the brains and Hungary the brawn in the empire?

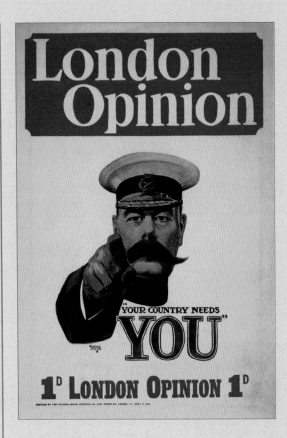

◀ Lord Kitchener's recruitment drive hugely bolstered British forces

6 THE FORTUNES OF THE BRITISH ARMY

In 1914, Britain had two armies – a domestic defence army, the part-time Territorial Force (TF), and the regular British Expeditionary Force (BEF), equipped to serve or fight overseas. Totalling 700,000 including reserves, these were the essential components with which the British went to war.

Initially, the all-volunteer BEF was dwarfed by the conscript armies of France and Germany, yet it performed brilliantly in the 1914 battles of Mons, Le Cateau and First Ypres, though sustaining huge casualties. In Britain, a mass 'New Army' of willing citizen volunteers collected and trained until 1916 – prompted by Kitchener's legendary 'Your Country Needs You' recruitment posters. Meanwhile, the Territorial Force were deployed to the trenches and first bloodied in the unsuccessful battle of Loos (September-October 1915), which caused Sir John French's downfall and Haig's elevation.

With burgeoning armies in France and elsewhere, conscription was introduced for the first time ever in January 1916. That Britain deployed four armies – the regular BEF, Territorials, Kitchener volunteers and conscripts – was symptomatic of an inability to co-ordinate manpower or recognise the needs of total war. The Somme was the first major battle involving the Kitchener volunteers, who included many Pals and Chums units. Despite the setbacks of 1 July 1916, by November they had matured, gaining invaluable experience that was applied first at Arras in April, then Third Ypres (July-November), 1917.

The British were worn out by Third Ypres/Passchendaele at the end of 1917, though unaware that their opponents were even more exhausted. In March 1918 the BEF weathered a series of crushing German offensives and then, at Amiens on 8 August, went on the attack. The subsequent 'Hundred Days' marked the finest moments of Haig's BEF, applying all their hard-learned lessons to triumph. Alas, 1918 is largely forgotten by the British public, who prefer to remember the disasters of the earlier years, such as Gallipoli or the first day on the Somme.

7 THE ART OF RECRUITMENT

Recruitment posters were used most extensively in Britain and its Empire, where enlistment was, uniquely, voluntary (though in Britain itself conscription began in January 1916). The war produced the most famous advertising campaign ever, with Lord Kitchener's pointing finger 'Your Country Needs You'

Posters set out to demonise the enemy, or blackmail readers into enlisting – 'Daddy, What Did You Do In the War?', a young boy playing with his toy soldiers asked of his embarrassed father. An Irish recruiting poster tried to shame men into volunteering: 'Will You Go, or Must I?' demanded a young lady of her man as Belgium burns in the background. Women started 'shaming' young civilian males with a white feather, suggesting they should be in uniform.

These messages were repeated in newspapers, whilst regimental bands paraded in many streets to recruit men. The music halls joined in, and several hit songs of 1914-15 were based on recruiting messages.'

The established churches also played their part. Anglican bishops and vicars put on uniform; Welsh ministers recruited more from the pulpit than did sergeants in their recruiting halls. In urban areas, meetings in town halls were held by civic worthies, keen to raise companies and battalions bearing their name, and in the euphoria of August-September 1914, a battalion of 1,000 men could be raised in a day. However, this paid no attention to workers whose occupations were vital to the war effort.

Many volunteered out of curiosity, with misplaced notions of glamour, or even to escape urban life. A surprising number of married middle class men with families also volunteered, perhaps out of patriotism. In their enthusiasm, the young and old lied about their age to join up.

Recruitment was extraordinarily successful. By the end of September 1914, over 750,000 men had enlisted; by January 1915, a million. In total, 2.67 million volunteered – roughly matching conscripts.

Daddy, what did YOU do in the Great War ?

▲ Posters such as this used emotional blackmail to persuade readers to enlist

8 THE OTTOMAN EMPIRE

The Ottoman Empire, whose last remnant is modern Turkey, was a centuries-old sprawl of different cultures and states in the Middle East and ringing the Black Sea. Long past its zenith as a major power, it was regarded as the "sick man of Europe".

Although the Ottoman Empire initially declared itself neutral, it was under pressure to side with Berlin. A military mission of 1913 had modernised the army and navy to German standards and resulted in a secret treaty, signed in August 1914. The minister of war, Enver Pasha, was

both pro-German and opportunistic: following Germany's early victories in Europe, he declared war against Russia on 28 October 1914. The Triple Entente (Allied Powers) responded likewise on 5 November.

The motivation was an opportunity for swift triumphs over neighbours and a way of avoiding imminent disintegration of the Ottoman Empire. However, it was only ever a pawn in German strategy, designed to keep Russia at bay.

Led by a Turkish officer corps, armies were raised by conscripting

men from the many vassal states – Albanians, Greeks, Bulgarians, Arabs and Jews – but they were often unreliable. For the Gallipoli campaign, Muslims from Constantinople (hitherto exempt) were conscripted, and Turkish historians describe the Dardenelles casualties as amounting to "burying a university" in the area.

The Empire mobilised 2.8 million, of whom 300,000 were killed in action, while 450,000 died of disease. Troops suffered from outmoded equipment, malnourishment and poor clothing – Ottoman soldiers often took great risks just to rob the British dead of their boots and even clothing, whilst more died from abysmal medical care than combat.

Turkey remains sensitive to this day about the mass deportation and systematic killing of its Armenian population during and after the war, resulting in a death toll of between 1 and 1.5 million. Ottoman Assyrians and Greeks were similarly targeted, each ethnic group losing about 750,000 lives. Best estimates place the total number of wartime deaths at five million, including 4.5 million civilians, who suffered through disease, starvation or genocide.

◄ The Ottoman Empire drew on resources from across its disparate territories

Russian troops crossing
the Carpathians during
the Galicia campaign

9 THE EASTERN FRONT

We think of the First World War only in terms of its Western Front, but Germany and Austro-Hungary (with their Bulgarian and Turkish allies) also fought a significant series of interrelated campaigns in the East. Whilst static trench warfare dominated in the West, this front was characterised by relatively mobile battles, using cavalry.

The Russians mobilised more efficiently than anticipated, initially fielding 1.2 million men commanded by the Tsar's cousin, Grand Duke Nicholas. Reflecting the feudal society that was Russia, the force was intensely hierarchical and frowned on initiative. As a consequence, commanders and industry were slow to grasp new technologies. Long after poison gas first appeared, for example, Russian soldiers had not been issued with respirators. Generally, they were poorly equipped, requiring quantity rather than quality.

Russia immediately invaded East Prussia and Austro-Hungarian Galicia in 1914. Although defeated at Tannenberg in August, the Russians under Brusilov had taken Galicia by the end of the year. The campaign carried on in the Carpathian Mountains through the winter, but 1915 saw Russia pushed out of both Galicia and eastern Poland.

Mobilising more men, Brusilov resumed the offensive in June 1916 and made progress before reaching stalemate in September. In August 1916, Romania attacked Hungary, but was countered after a month of success by German-Austro-Bulgar forces, including mountain troops led by the young Rommel.

Then in, 1917, the Russian economy collapsed. Food shortages caused unrest, and the growing casualties also served to create disaffection, leading to Lenin's seizure of power in November. He immediately sought an end to the conflict, signing the Treaty of Brest-Litovsk in March 1918.

The vast bureaucracy of Imperial Russia consistently mismanaged her campaigning, and Russian statistics reflect this: the records were so poor that we do not know her final death toll. Sources vary between one and two million killed, including 400,000 to 900,000 dying of wounds and disease, reflecting the appalling state of Russian military medicine. Up to four million were captured, indicating their unwillingness to fight.

10 THE RISE OF AIR POWER

The war's earliest military aviation was naval, used for fleet reconnaissance and, throughout, the most important air mission remained intelligence gathering. New technologies helped, such as photographic film and wireless telegraphy. On land, this meant it was essential to conceal everything from airborne eyes, making camouflage a necessity.

This prompted the need to destroy enemy scouts while protecting one's own, giving rise to air-to-air combat. Initially, pilots and observers duelled with personal firearms. In 1915, aeroplanes became weapons when Anton Fokker, a Dutch engineer working in Germany, invented the interrupter gear, allowing machine guns to shoot through a propeller.

Pilots became popular figures of mythic proportions, partly because of the sheer romantic improbability of flight, but also because they restored an element of single combat to the anonymous slaughter of modern war. Pilots with five 'kills' became aces, and their chivalric image survived long after air tactics slid into deadly routine.

The ability to attack tactical targets became important, but the potential to deliver strategic destruction was realised only slowly. Besides zeppelins, heavy bombers emerged late in the war, with large, multi-engine bombers capable of lifting up to a ton of explosives – Handley-Pages and German Gothas. Cities were attacked, causing many casualties. By 1918, huge resources were devoted to anti-aircraft artillery ('Archie', later called 'Flak') and barrage balloons.

On 1 April 1918, the RAF emerged out of the Army's Royal Flying Corps (RFC) and the Royal Navy Air Service (RNAS) – the world's first independent air force. For Hugh Trenchard, its boss, independence allowed exploration of all possibilities, without being held hostage to terrestrial doctrines. In Ludendorff's offensive of March 1918, German squadrons directly supported infantry, and helped achieve a decisive breakthrough. Thus, when imitated successfully by the Allies at Amiens in August, command of the air did not make victory on land unnecessary, but made it possible. Whilst Germany stayed ahead technologically, superiority in the air ultimately rested with the side possessing greater resources and the ability to out-build opponents.

▶▶▶ BRITAIN'S FLYING ACES – PAGE 82

▲ 1 April 1918: a fighter of 22 Squadron flies over the Vert Galand aerodrome, France, on the RAF's inauguration day

▲ British soldiers unleash their Vickers machine gun during the Battle of the Somme: the machine gun revolutionised warfare

11 THE EVOLUTION OF THE MACHINE GUN

The Prussian Army learned the value of machine guns when they encountered a single French *mitrailleuse* at Gravelotte on 18 August 1870, which caused over 2,500 casualties. This lesson was never forgotten and by 1914 the Germans understood better than anyone their defensive potential, using overlapping arcs of fire as a block to advancing troops.

Hiram Maxim's water-cooled machine-gun was demonstrated to British staff officers in 1885. Capable of 600 rounds per minute, Maxim guns were first bought by the British in 1889 and first issued to infantry battalions in 1891. By 1899 Germany had also adopted them, as had Russia. Both these nations manufactured them under licence, and Russia first employed its 7.62mm Maxims with devastating effect in the Russo-Japanese War of 1904.

In 1914, both Britain and Germany went to war with versions of the Maxim: the 0.303-inch British Vickers Mk. 1 and the German 7.92mm MaschinenGewehr (MG) Model 1908. The Vickers weighed 34lbs and the MG-08 44lbs, without their tripods. The French used the 8mm air-cooled Hotchkiss, which weighed, with tripod, 110lbs. In the USA, Browning continued the development of machine guns, eventually producing the 0.30-06-inch water-cooled Model 1917, which came into service in France in 1918.

Manoeuvrability in tight trenches forced the design of light versions, the British adopting the American Lewis and the Germans modifying the MG-08 in 1915 by fitting a shoulder stock and bipod, and designating it the MG-08/15. Both weapons, though lighter than the Vickers or MG-08, were still cumbersome.

Tripods – though heavy – gave stability, which brought range and predictability. All these guns could reach beyond 2,000 yards, and indirect fire techniques were developed for multiple guns, like artillery, as well as the obvious direct fire tactics. As the supreme defensive weapon, the machine gun effectively created the stalemate of trench warfare, before being countered by the tank.

GETTY X3

12 ADOLF HITLER'S FORMATIVE YEARS

Hitler's life was transformed by the Great War. Ironically, he had moved to Germany in 1913 to avoid conscription into the Austro-Hungarian army, but a photograph exists of the future Führer among a joyful crowd in Munich welcoming war in 1914 (see below).

Perhaps soldiering gave him a sense of identity – it certainly provided his life with structure, hierarchy and a family. His new 'home' became the 16th Bavarian Reserve Regiment.

After two months of training, the regiment was thrown against the British at Gheluvelt, near Ypres, on 29 October 1914. Hitler emerged unharmed, though the unit lost 2,500 of its 3,000 soldiers. He narrowly escaped death several times, providing the sense of 'divine intervention' that later sustained him. On 7 October 1916, Hitler's luck ran out when he sustained a leg wound near Bapaume on the Somme This injury saw him hospitalised back in Germany.

Serving mainly as a battalion runner, on 31 July 1918 he received the Iron Cross 1st Class, recommended by his Jewish officer, Oberleutnant Hugo Gutmann. That October, Hitler was partially blinded in a gas attack near Ypres. Sent to a military hospital, he was convalescing when news of the 11 November 1918 Armistice reached him.

Never promoted beyond corporal, and with no training for leadership or high command, he arguably spent the rest of his days re-living the period of his life he found most fulfilling: making war.

The Treaty of Versailles, with its harsh penalties on Germany, triggered widespread resentment, which Hitler was able to exploit with a sense that Germany must regain its lost honour. This partly accounts for his rise to power and appeal to the military.

His many biographers agree that without the Great War, there would have been no Hitler. It made him as a person and its aftermath provided him with a route to power.

▲ Adolf Hitler joins the crowds outside the Odeonplatz during the mobilisation of the German army

The *Lusitania*
was sunk by a
German torpedo,
despite being
full of civilian
passengers

13 THE SINKING OF THE *LUSITANIA*

At 31,550 gross tons, the four-funnelled *Lusitania* was the flagship passenger liner of the Cunard Line, the *Titanic* of its day. A floating luxury hotel launched in 1907, she was the fastest and largest liner on the transatlantic run.

Whilst crossing from New York to Southampton on 7 May 1915, she was hit off the southern coast of Ireland by a lone torpedo fired without warning by the U-20, sinking in 18 minutes. She took with her 1,198 passengers and crew, including 128 neutral Americans.

exploited the event for their own ends, for at stake was the intervention of the United States – hitherto neutral – into the war.

Germany emphasised that newspaper advertisements in the US had warned passengers of the perils of sailing in wartime, but more importantly that *Lusitania* had virtually exploded on being hit, as though she was carrying ammunition. Great Britain highlighted the fact that U-20 had fired without warning and that over 1,000 defenceless civilians had died,

In fact, she was carrying ammunition and gun cotton, which in theory made her a legitimate naval target, but recent marine archaeology has revealed that whilst she may have been conveying over 4 million US-manufactured 0.303-inch rifle cartridges, it was coal dust in her near-empty bunkers that detonated and blew out her sides, triggered by U-20's torpedo. Nevertheless, it was aggressive acts like the attack on the *Lusitania* that prompted President Woodrow Wilson to declare war on Germany

14 DOUGLAS HAIG: HERO OR VILLAIN?

As architect of the massive and costly offensives of the Somme (1916) and Third Ypres (1917), historians remain split as to whether Haig deserves censure for those offensives, or praise for the victory achieved in 1918. However, it is difficult to blame him for the four inconclusive years his men spent in the trenches: technology, not Haig, forced them there.

Haig was the product of an educational system that worshipped sport and put character before intellect. Though often portrayed as intellectually dull, his three years at Brasenose College, Oxford (1880-83) and two at Staff College (1896-7), suggest otherwise. They trained him to see that superior character should always prevail in war.

Yet he was also a progressive spirit who sponsored reform of the army from 1906-09, and the introduction of new technologies, such as machine guns, mortars, gas, aircraft and tanks.

When appointed Commander in Chief of the BEF in December 1915, he was certain of his worthiness and confident he knew how to win. This self-assurance was reinforced by his religious faith: he certainly cared about his men, contrary to the barbs of his many critics. Influenced by his chief intelligence officer, John Charteris, he believed from the autumn of 1916, that the Germans were on the verge of collapse, and therefore susceptible to a knockout blow.

Haig's challenge was that his army grew to over two million men, for which neither he nor his generals had any preparation. He answered his country's call and did what he had been trained to do. In the Victorian age that would have made him a hero, but when the whole nation went to war, victory became redefined: it was no longer enough just to

▲ Has history been unfair to Field Marshal Sir Douglas Haig?

win. Haig was educated in the ideals of one age but judged by the standards of another.

▶▶▶ DOUGLAS HAIG – PAGE 66

15 CHURCHILL STEPS UP

The future Prime Minister had more experience of military operations than almost any other British politician, passing out from Sandhurst in 1894. He managed to combine the role of army officer and war correspondent in the 17th Lancers at one of the last cavalry charges, Omdurman in 1898.

The next year found him in South Africa, where he was captured by Boers when the armoured train in which he was travelling was ambushed. He later escaped confinement and achieved fame worldwide as a result.

Churchill entered Parliament as MP for Oldham in 1900 and by 1911 was in the Cabinet as First Lord of the Admiralty, promoting naval aviation (taking flying lessons) and switching the Navy from coal to oil. In 1914 he mobilized the fleet, founded the Royal Naval Division and later oversaw the development of the tank, which was financed from naval research funds.

As one of the architects of the 1915 Gallipoli landings, he shouldered the blame for the subsequent fiasco, and resigned from the Government on 12 November. Remaining an MP, in a characteristic gesture of bravery (perhaps tinged with a suicidal death wish), he departed for the Western Front, attached to the Grenadier Guards, and on 5 January 1916 took command of the 6th Battalion, Royal Scots Fusiliers.

He saw action, was shelled, and his section of the front near Ypres at Ploegsteert lay not far from the German held town of Messines, where Corporal Adolf Hitler was serving. Two future Prime Ministers, Eden and Macmillan, also shared his experience of the trenches.

In 1916, restless away from the House of Commons, he returned to England, and a year later (July 1917) joined Lloyd George's administration as Minister of Munitions. His six-volume political-strategic history of the war, *The World Crisis*, was published between 1923-31, to critical acclaim.

◀ Winston Churchill (centre) photographed in France, 1916

▶▶▶ *Turn to page 42 to learn how battles such as Gallipoli, Verdun, the Somme and Passchendaele contribute to* The Story of the War

Austrian crown prince Franz Ferdinand and his wife, Sophie, leave Sarajevo City Hall on 28 June 1914. Five minutes later, the couple were fatally shot

(Below) British newspaper the *Daily Chronicle* reports the events

Daily C

LONDON, MONDAY, JUNE 29.

NO. 4,438.

HEIR TO AUSTRIAN THRONE MURDERED.

ARCHDUKE AND HIS WIFE SHOT DEAD IN THE STREET.

DETERMINED PLOT.

BOMB FIRST THROWN AT THEIR CAR.

The Shots Heard Around The World

The assassination of Archduke Franz Ferdinand in 1914 famously triggered the First World War. And, as **Christopher Clark** argues, it's an event still loaded with sharp resonance for our current times

On the morning of Sunday 28 June 1914, Archduke Franz Ferdinand, heir apparent to the Austro-Hungarian throne, and his wife Countess Sophie Chotek von Chotkowa und Wognin arrived by train in the city of Sarajevo and joined a motorcade for the ride to City Hall. A picturesque view unfolded before the couple as the motorcade swung onto the Appel Quay, driving eastward along the river.

Sarajevo lies in a narrow valley watered by the Miljačka, which gushes from a gorge just above the town. On either side, steep hills rise towards the clouds. The hillsides were speckled with villas and houses standing in orchards. Further up were the cemeteries with their glowing dots of white marble, crowned by dark firs and buffs of naked rock.

The minarets of numerous mosques could be seen rising from among the trees and buildings along the river, a reminder of the city's Ottoman past. The previous day had been cool and rainy but,

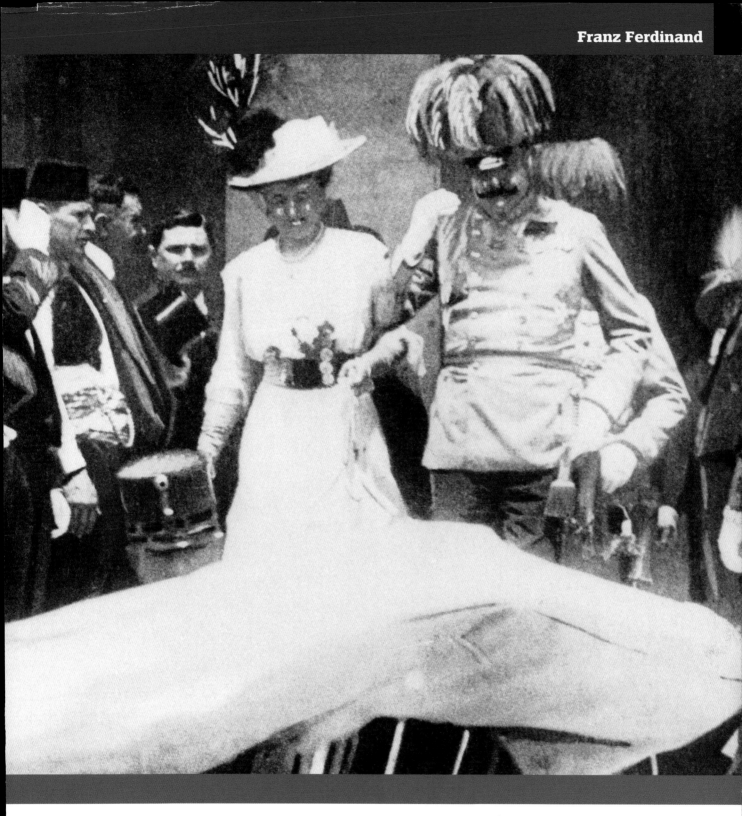

on the morning of 28 June, the city was bathed in hot sunshine.

But, during the days preceding the visit, seven terrorists, organised into two cells, had gathered in the city. On the morning of the Archduke's arrival, they positioned themselves at intervals along the quay, a broad boulevard running along the embankment of the Miljačka River through the centre of Sarajevo. Strapped around their waists were bombs no bigger than cakes of soap with detonator caps and 12-second chemical fuses. In their pockets were loaded revolvers.

The manpower was essential to the success of the undertaking. If one man were searched and arrested or simply failed to act, another stood by to take his place.

Strapped around the terrorists' waists were bombs the size of cakes of soap. In their pockets were loaded revolvers

Each carried a paper packet of cyanide powder so that he could take his own life when the deed was done.

Of the seven would-be assassins, only two carried out their instructions. The first to go into action was Nedeljko Čabrinović, who had placed himself on the river side of the quay. He freed his bomb, broke the detonator against a lamp-post and threw it at the passing car. The bomb missed its mark, fell to the ground and exploded beneath the car ▷

An engraving in Italian newspaper *La Domenica del Corriere* shows Gavrilo Princip gunning down the royal couple after their car had mistakenly turned into Franz Joseph Street

▷ behind, wounding several of the officers inside and gouging a hole in the road.

The Archduke responded to this mishap with astonishing sang froid. "Come on," he said, "that fellow is clearly insane; let us proceed with our programme." The motorcade lurched back into motion, with the rear-most drivers picking their way around the smoking wreck of the third car. The remaining assassins, still waiting at their posts, were thus given every opportunity to complete their task. But they were young and inexperienced and most of them lost their nerve when the car and its passengers came within range.

Gavrilo Princip, the best marksman of the seven, was at first caught off guard. Hearing the bomb explode, he assumed that the plot had already succeeded. He ran towards Čabrinović's position, only to see him being borne away by his captors, bent over in agony as the poison burned his throat. "I immediately saw that he had not succeeded and that he had not been able to poison himself," Princip later revealed. "I intended to shoot him quickly with my revolver. At this moment, the cars drove by."

Change of plan

Princip abandoned the plan to kill his accomplice and turned his attention to the motorcade, but by the time he could see the Archduke – unmistakeable in his helmet adorned with brilliant green ostrich feathers – the car was moving too fast for him to get a clear shot. Princip stayed calm, an extraordinary feat under the circumstances. Realising that the couple would soon be on their return journey, he took up a new position on the right side of Franz Joseph Street, along the publicly advertised route by which the motorcade was to leave the city.

The ceremonial formalities at City Hall went off without a hitch, though witnesses later recalled

that the Archduke appeared increasingly nervous.

In order to avoid further attacks, it was agreed that the party should drive straight back down the Appel Quay rather than up Franz Joseph Street, as any further prospective assassin would presumably be expecting. But no-one thought to inform the drivers of the changed itinerary. The lead car swung to the right into Franz Joseph Street and the car carrying Franz Ferdinand and Sophie made to follow.

This was Gavrilo Princip's moment. He had positioned himself in front of a shop on the right side of Franz Joseph Street and caught up with the car as it slowed almost to a stop. Unable to disentangle the bomb tied to his waist in time, he drew his revolver instead and fired twice from point-blank range into the open passenger compartment. Time – as we know from Princip's later testimony – seemed to slow as he left the shade of the shop awnings to take aim. The sight of the duchess gave him momentary pause. "As I saw that a lady was sitting next to him, I reflected for a moment whether to shoot or not. At the same time, I was filled with a peculiar feeling…"

The recollection of General Potiorek, who was seated in the second car with the two victims, conveys a similar sense of unreality. Potiorek remembered sitting stock still, gazing into the face of the killer as the shots were fired, but seeing no smoke or muzzle flash and hearing only muted shots that seemed to come from far away.

At first, it seemed as if the shooter had missed his mark, because Franz Ferdinand and his wife remained motionless and upright in their seats. In reality, they were both already dying. The first bullet had passed through the door of the carriage into the Duchess's abdomen, severing the stomach artery; the second had hit the Archduke in the neck, tearing the jugular vein. As the car ▷

> **Unable to disentangle the bomb, Princip drew his revolver, firing twice from point-blank range**

Serbian troops inspect a row of cannons during the First Balkan War, 1912

BALKAN POWDER KEG
How the region was already volatile before the Sarajevo assassinations

The Balkan Wars began in Africa. In the autumn of 1911, Italy launched a war of conquest on Tripolitania, a North African province of the Ottoman Empire, triggering a chain of opportunist assaults on Ottoman territories across the Balkans. In October 1912, a loose coalition of states – Serbia, Montenegro, Bulgaria and Greece – mounted parallel invasions of the Balkan lands of the Ottoman Empire, thereby starting the First Balkan War (October 1912-May 1913). The result was a momentous victory for the Balkan allies over the Ottoman forces, who were driven out of Albania, Macedonia and Thrace.

In the Second Balkan War (June-July 1913), the belligerents fought over the spoils of the first: Serbia, Montenegro, Greece and Romania fought Bulgaria for territories in Macedonia, Thrace and the Dobrudja respectively.

These cruel conflicts transformed the geopolitics of south-eastern Europe. The kingdom of Serbia's territory nearly doubled; its population grew by more than 1.5 million. Three hundred thousand Serbian troops had been put into the field within three weeks of the first mobilisation order in October 1912. The 'reunification' of the 'Serb lands' (including Bosnia and Herzegovina, provinces of the Austro-Hungarian monarchy) remained a political goal of primary importance. Austria-Hungary thus faced a new and threatening constellation on its south-eastern periphery.

The retreat of Ottoman power troubled Russia. If Ottoman power on the Bosphorus collapsed, who would inherit control of the strategically vital Turkish Straits? Concern over these issues heightened the tension between Vienna and St Petersburg during the last 18 months before the outbreak of war. The two continental alliance blocs were drawn deeper into the antipathies of a region that was entering a period of unprecedented volatility.

The heir and his family: Archduke Franz Ferdinand with his wife Sophie and (l-r) their children Ernst, Maximilian and Sophie

▷ roared away from the scene, the Duchess teetered sideways until her face was between her husband's knees. Potiorek initially thought she had fainted with shock. Only when he saw blood issuing from the Archduke's mouth did he realise something more serious was afoot. Franz Ferdinand's bodyguard, Count von Harrach, heard the premier speaking, in a soft voice, words that would become famous throughout the world: "Sophie, Sophie, don't die. Stay alive for our children!"

Sophie was dead by the time the party reached the Konak, the Governor's residence; Franz Ferdinand was comatose. The couple were rushed into rooms on the first floor. The Archduke's valet, Count Morsey, who had run all the way from the scene of the shooting to rejoin the Archduke, tried to ease his breathing by cutting his uniform open at the front. Blood splashed up, staining the yellow cuffs of the valet's uniform.

Morsey asked Franz Ferdinand if he had a message for his children, but there was no reply – the Archduke's lips were already stiffening. It was a matter of minutes before those present agreed that the heir apparent was dead. It was 11am. Bells began tolling across the city.

In the second half of the 20th century, a kind of period charm accumulated around the events of 1914. It was easy to imagine the disaster of Europe's 'last summer' as an Edwardian costume drama. The effete rituals and gaudy uniforms, the 'ornamentalism' of a world still largely organised around hereditary monarchy had a distancing effect on present-day recollection. They seemed to signal that the protagonists were people from another, vanished world. The presumption stealthily asserted itself that if the actors' hats had gaudy green ostrich feathers on them, then their thoughts and motivations probably did too.

Raw modernity

Yet what must strike any 21st-century reader who follows the course of the summer crisis of 1914 is its raw modernity. It began with a squad of suicide bombers and a cavalcade of automobiles. Behind the outrage at Sarajevo was the Black Hand, an avowedly terrorist organisation with a cult of sacrifice, death and revenge. But this terrorist organisation was extra-territorial,

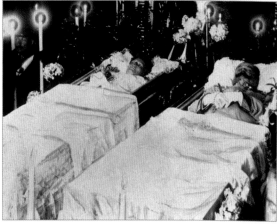

▲ Franz Ferdinand and Duchess Sophie lie in state following their assassinations

without a clear geographical or political location. Scattered in cells across political borders, it was unaccountable, its links to any sovereign government were oblique, hidden and difficult to discern from outside the organisation.

Indeed, one could even say that July 1914 is much less remote from us – less illegible – now than it was in the 1980s. Since the end of the Cold War, a system of global bipolar stability has made way for a more complex and unpredictable array of forces, including declining empires and rising powers – inviting comparison with Europe in 1914.

The Yugoslav wars of the 1990s have since reminded us of the lethality of Balkan nationalism. Since the Srebrenica massacre and the siege of Sarajevo, it has become harder to think of Serbia as the mere object or victim of great power politics and easier to conceive of Serbian nationalism as an historical force in its own right. From the perspective of the new Europe, we are inclined to look more sympathetically – or at least less contemptuously – than we used to on the vanished imperial patchwork of Habsburg Austria-Hungary. These shifts in perspective prompt us to rethink the story of how war came to Europe in 1914, not by embracing a vulgar presentism that remakes the past to meet the needs of the present, but rather by acknowledging those features of the past of which our changed vantage point can afford us a clearer view.

Among these is the Balkan context of the war's inception. Of the seven assassins, six were ethnic Serbs. Three (including Princip and Čabrinović) had only recently crossed the border from Serbia, where they had been supplied with bombs, guns and poison of Serbian manufacture. Princip had been trained in marksmanship by a Black Hand agent in a park outside Belgrade. And there were links between the Black Hand and parts of the Serbian state, whose

leader, Prime Minister Nikola Pašić, appears to have possessed foreknowledge of the attack.

Yet Serbia remains one of the blind spots in the historiography of the July Crisis. The assassination is treated in many accounts as a mere pretext, an event with little bearing on the real forces whose interaction brought war. The truth is that it confronted the Austro-Hungarian authorities with a challenge they were unable to ignore. To convey a sense of the gravity of the situation as they saw it, we need merely ask ourselves how the United States would respond today to the assassination of a president-elect and his wife by a Tehran-trained hit squad.

Explaining how the assassinations – and the Austrian response to them – triggered the cascade of decisions that produced a continental war is another matter. But the assassinations remind us of the power that a single, symbolic event – however deeply it may be enmeshed in larger processes – can wield over history. Just as with the attack on the World Trade Centre in September 2001, the Sarajevo murders changed politics, rendering old options obsolete and endowing new ones with an unforeseen urgency. ◨

> ## The assassinations remind us of the power that a single, symbolic event can wield on world history

Christopher Clark's latest book is *The Sleepwalkers: How Europe Went To War In 1914* (Allen Lane, 2012)

The First World War's early shots are fired by a Serbian heavy artillery battery in July 1914

THE ESCALATION OF WAR
How events in the Balkans drew the rest of Europe into bloody conflict

The First World War was the Third Balkan War before it became the First World War. How was this possible? Conflicts and crises on the south-eastern periphery, where the Ottoman Empire abutted Christian Europe, were nothing new. In the course of the Balkan Wars, however, the conflicts of the Balkan theatre became tightly intertwined with the geopolitics of the European system during the summer of 1914.

Austria, which had once dismissed the Serbs as "rascally boys" stealing apples from the Habsburg orchard, adopted an increasingly militant view of the Balkan situation. The hawks spoke with ever louder voices and the leading Austrian dove, Archduke Franz Ferdinand, would perish in Sarajevo in June 1914.

Equally important was Russia's deepening support for Serbia, now the dominant Slavic power of the Balkan region. In Paris, French President Raymond Poincaré extended the remit of the Franco-Russian alliance, assuring French support if Russia felt obliged to aid Serbia by waging war on Austria-Hungary. Should this eventuality arise, a continental war was highly likely; Germany's treaty commitments to Vienna would be triggered by a Russian mobilisation, while its military planning foresaw parallel mobilisations against both France and Russia.

British policy-makers viewed these developments with ambivalence. The remoteness of the Balkan theatre made it difficult for Foreign Secretary Edward Grey to persuade the Cabinet and public that British intervention was warranted. Only by shifting the focus of the discussion westwards to the issue of Belgian neutrality and Britain's 'moral' commitment to France was Grey able to make a case for committing Britain to the war.

> Read more about the origins of the First World War on the BBC website ➜ **bbc.in/QyUeii**

▲ Blood on their hands: Gavrilo Princip (left) pictured in 1912, two years before that fateful June day in Sarajevo. Ivo Kranjčević (centre) hid the weapons of one of the assassins. Nedeljko Čabrinović (right) threw a bomb at the Archduke

The Tommy's view

In an article previously published in *BBC History Magazine*, the late military historian **Richard Holmes** explains how soldiers dealt with life in the trenches

HOW DID THEY COPE WITH THE HORROR?

"The most dreadful picture in my Somme gallery is a landscape – a wide upland slope, uniformly drab, dirty white, chalk mixed with decaying vegetation, nor a tree stump or bush left, just desolation, with a track named Crucifix Alley for men to walk round or through shell holes to the larger desolation of Delville Wood. The whole blasted slope clotted to the very edges with dead bodies, too many to bury, and too costly, the area being under constant fire from artillery. This awful display of dead men looked like a set piece, as though some celestial undertaker had spaced the corpses evenly for interment and then been interrupted. Several times I picked my way through this cemetery of the unburied. A landscape picture my memory turns up in horror."

Second Lieutenant Bernard Martin, North Staffordshires

Landscape of death: bodies litter the road after the Battle of the Aisne in 1917. Enemy fire often prevented soldiers from burying the dead

Richard Holmes The average Tommy would see dreadful things, but not every day. It isn't generally understood that soldiers were rotated through from rest and reserve to the front line and back. They had the opportunity to psyche themselves up and wind themselves down. They played mind games on themselves. They could cope with the switchback by thinking, 'We're going up the line tonight – it's going to be awful, but actually this time next week I'll be back, and then God knows what'll happen.' We have to remember that they weren't like us – theirs was a generation used to seeing death, used to seeing siblings die of diseases that would now be preventable. They were tougher because they generally speaking came from a harsher environment. For many, it wasn't as much of a shock as we might think. We would find it far tougher today. Our expectations have grown and we're less deferential, more questioning. This was a generation built to endure.

Commander-in-chief Douglas Haig (above) was heavily criticised, but Tommies were more worried about how good their battalion commander was

WHAT DID THEY THINK OF THEIR COMMANDERS?

"The want of preparation, the vague orders, the ignorance of the objective and geography, the absurd haste, and in general the horrid bungling were scandalous. After two years of war it seems that our higher commanders are still without common sense. In any well-regulated organisation a divisional commander would be shot for incompetence – here another regiment is ordered to attempt the same task in the same maddening way."

Quartermaster Sergeant Scott Macfie, King's Liverpool Regiment

Richard Holmes If you went to Tommy and said 'What do you think of high command?', he'd neither know nor care. He was more concerned with his immediate world, and that's circumscribed by the battalion – 1,000 men commanded by a lieutenant colonel. That was his little world.

He probably wouldn't have known the divisional commander by name. He'd have known who the commander-in-chief was, but he probably wouldn't have had an opinion. You'll get people in letters and diaries who are critical at the time, but it's far less than you'd expect. This is not an army that particularly believes itself to be an army of lions commanded by donkeys.

GETTY X4

WHAT DID THEY THINK OF THE ENEMY?

'I came face to face with a great big German who had come up unexpectedly out of a shell hole. He had his rifle and bayonet at the ready. So had I, but mine suddenly felt only the size of a small boy's play gun and my steel helmet shrank to the size of a small tin lid. Then, almost before I had time to realise what was happening, the German threw down his rifle, put up his arms and shouted 'Kamerad'. I could hardly believe my eyes.'

*Lance Corporal F Heardman,
2/Manchester Palsw*

German soldiers in the trenches in 1914. Tommies thought they were simply on the wrong side rather than intrinsically evil

Richard Holmes Generally speaking, the Germans were regarded as a firm but fair opponent. They were wrong, because they were on the wrong side, but they were not thought to be bad blokes. A lot of people spoke very well of German NCOs. At a personal level, Tommy and Fritz (and it was always Tommy and Fritz) got on quite well when one was a prisoner of the other.

There was not much hatred, but there were exceptions. Once the Germans had used gas, for example, German POWs were not treated well. Units and individuals had needle matches. In other words, an individual might have lost a relative, and thereafter he would have been disinclined to take prisoners; equally, a unit might have felt that it was badly treated by the Germans on a particular occasion and it would have felt disinclined to take prisoners.

Gassed French infantrymen escorted by British soldiers after the Battle of Marne, 1918

HOW BAD WAS THE GAS?

'The scene that followed was heartbreaking. Men were caught by the fumes and in dreadful agony, coughing and vomiting, rolling on the ground in agony…I ran around at intervals and tied up a lot of men's mouths, placed them in sitting positions and organised parties to assist them to the support dugouts…when we found our men were dying from fumes we wanted to charge, but were not allowed to do so. What a start for May. Hell could find no worse [than] the groans of scores of dying and badly hurt men.'

*Sergeant Major Ewwst Shephard,
1/Dorsets*

Richard Holmes Gas is one of those things that in a strange way defined the war. It wasn't actually a big killer – it wounded far more than it killed. One of the very vivid images is of someone in the 1920s and 1930s coughing and spluttering because he'd been gassed in the First World War. It's that enduring image, not of the soldier killed by gas, but of the soldier who's been touched by gas and who carries it with him for the rest of his life as a dreadful coughing memento of the war.

There is something about gas that goes to the heart of the question of endurance. Being gassed is no more qualitatively awful than being blown apart by a shell, but there is something about gas that saps courage. There was a feeling that it was a piece of devilry. Even if you didn't see it kill lots of your friends, you had this feeling that there was something nasty, underhand and subhuman about gas.

Richard Holmes, who passed away in 2011, presented numerous history programmes on the BBC network. The veterans' quotes used here are taken from his book *Tommy: The British Soldier On The Western Front 1914-1918* (HarperCollins, 2004)

BBC

TOPFOTO

Admiral Charlton reviews
troops of the King's African
Rifles during a parade in Lindi,
Tanzania, September 1916

THE EMPIRE AT WAR

Britain's declaration of war brought millions of its colonial subjects into the conflict and few corners of its Empire were left unscathed, as **Ashley Jackson** explains

It is unsurprising that images of the Western Front dominate British popular memory of the First World War, given the proximity of the trenches to British homes and the fact that the majority of British war dead perished just across the Channel.

Britain's 1914-18 war experience, however, was as much about imperial conflict as it was about the trenches. As the world's foremost imperial power, Britain's declaration of war in August 1914 brought hundreds of millions of colonial subjects into conflict with Germany. Mobilisation of the Empire presented Britain with the opportunity to draw upon a massive reserve of military resources. Yet it also gave the Germans an opportunity: to follow the example of Britain's past foes and to target the Empire's many frontiers and lines of communication.

Australians, Egyptians, Indians, Iraqis, Kenyans, Namibians and Sri Lankans all fought and fell in the First World War – and the fact that the conflict means anything at all to people in such disparate lands is testament to the fact that it was a global struggle. The manner and the places in which the British fought the war, together with the strategic aims of the government, all bore the unmistakeable

hallmarks of Britain's imperial lineage. Infantry slogging matches in the shadow of Mount Kilimanjaro, or dusty campaigning in the land of Lawrence of Arabia, were far more than exotic and terrible sideshows to the slaughter in Europe. Similarly, the naval war was a global vigil on the part of the Royal Navy and its Dominion branches, involving ceaseless patrol and escort work as well as gun duels.

Mobilisation of the Empire gave Britain a massive reserve from which to draw military resources

Just as hundreds of thousands of imperial troops fought in Europe, so much of the First World War's action took place in imperial theatres. Australia and New Zealand conquered German Pacific territories such as German Samoa, Papua New Guinea and the Bismarck Archipelago. A British Indian army surrendered to Turkish forces at Kut in Mesopotamia (now Iraq) as it attempted to capture Baghdad.

Indian Army and Allied Japanese troops captured the German enclave of Tsingtao on

▲ An Indian soldier serving with the British Army observes the German trenches using a periscope

the Chinese coast, home of the German navy in the east. Jan Smuts and Louis Botha led a South African army of over 60,000 men into German South West Africa in 1915, while Trinidadians and Guianans in the British West Indies Regiment fought in Jordan, Mesopotamia and Palestine.

Duty to the King
In East Africa, the German guerrilla commander Colonel Paul Von Lettow Vorbeck bogged down a 300,000-strong British imperial force in a debilitating campaign that spanned Kenya, Tanganyika, Nyasaland and Northern Rhodesia, before finally surrendering nearly six weeks after the Armistice.

Elsewhere, the war persuaded the British to invade the sultanate of Darfur and incorporate it into Anglo-Egyptian Sudan, for fear of it falling under Ottoman sway. And classic big gun actions were fought in the Pacific and the South Atlantic, while the Germans preyed on merchant ships with surface raiders and submarines in order to sever trade lifelines.

The First World War was notably imperial in terms of its higher management. By 1914, a Committee of Imperial Defence had been established and the Dominions had some input into decision-making. In 1917, Prime Minister David Lloyd George formed an Imperial War Cabinet, on which Dominions leaders sat when visiting London, notably the fiery Welsh Prime Minister of Australia, William Morris Hughes. This was an incredible form of coalition government and an expression of common imperial identity binding British communities from Vancouver to the Tasman Sea. ▷

▲ German midget submarines and U-boats attacked Empire trade routes

HOW THE EMPIRE CAME TO BRITAIN'S AID

1 Canada
Canada recruited 628,964 soldiers, serving in Western Europe and the Middle East. Newfoundland recruited 11,922 men, including a special forestry unit.

2 Ireland
Despite its troubled relationship with Britain, Ireland during the First World War was still a part of the British Empire and 134,202 Irishmen were recruited into the army from all over the island and across the religious divide.

3 Middle East
A vast number of Egyptians were recruited into British labour battalions. A Zion Mule Corps supported a British division at Gallipoli, while Jews from the US, Britain, Canada and Palestine formed battalions of the City of London Regiment.

4 India
The Indian Army was 239,561 strong at the war's start. Between 1914 and 1918, its ranks were swelled by a further 1,161,789 recruits. They served in France, East Africa, Mesopotamia, Egypt, Gallipoli, Salonica, Palestine, Aden and the Persian Gulf.

5 West Indies
The British West Indian colonies sent over 10,000 men to fight for the Allied cause in the war.

The employment of personnel
A breakdown of where British and Empire soldiers of the Great War fought and fell...

German South West Africa, Togo and the Cameroons, North Russia and Vladivostok, and Australasia

France

East Africa

Egypt and Palestine

Mesopotamia

Dardanelles

Salonica

Italy

6 East Africa
The King's African Rifles, drawn from Nyasaland, Kenya and Uganda, rose in strength from 2,400 in 1914 to 34,000 by 1918. Hundreds of thousands of Africans acted as porters for imperial forces in the East African campaign.

7 Ceylon
Ceylon provided a 237-strong contingent of the Ceylon Planters Rifle Corps, deployed in the defence of the Suez Canal and at Gallipoli. Over 1,000 other men from Ceylon were recruited for the British Army's Sanitary Corps.

8 South Africa
South Africa recruited 136,070 white and 92,837 non-white soldiers, including a 30,000- strong South African Native Labour Contingent containing men recruited in the British protectorates of Basutoland, Bechuanaland, and Swaziland.

9 Mauritius
Seventeen hundred Mauritians were sent to Mesopotamia to work on the waterways of the Euphrates and the Tigris, while 500 Franco-Mauritians fought on the Western Front.

10 Australia and New Zealand
Australia recruited 416,809 soldiers and New Zealand 120,099. ANZACs served in Egypt, Palestine, France, Gallipoli, Samoa and other Pacific islands. Fiji recruited a labour battalion for service in France.

▷ A number of renowned imperial proconsuls, academics and statesmen buttressed the imperial view of the war in the British government. Lloyd George and Winston Churchill were noted for their interest in Britain's imperial affairs and many senior British imperialists were encamped in and around Downing Street, including Arthur Balfour, George Curzon, Alfred Milner, Lionel Curtis, Philip Kerr, Leopold Amery and the novelist John Buchan.

These guardians of Empire were determined that the 'southern world' would be secured as a result of the war, which meant Britain retaining German colonies in the Pacific, East Africa and Southern Africa, dominating the land bridge between Europe and India and securing the oil reserves of the Gulf once and for all.

The war was further marked as an imperial conflict by British territories around the world considering it the most momentous political event of their age, no matter how far they were from Germany. Settlers from New Zealand to Canada, from the highlands of Kenya to the streets of Bulawayo, shared the urge to publicly demonstrate their loyalty to Britain.

Just as importantly, the people over whom the Europeans ruled were told that it was their war; the elites of colonial society took this as a cue to support the war effort. They did this through raising money and recruiting men, donating sugar and rum to the British government, raising funds to buy military aircraft, and subscribing to charitable funds for widowed women or wounded seamen.

Settlers from New Zealand to Canada shared the urge to publicly demonstrate their loyalty to Britain

The rhetoric of imperial loyalty was spoken as a common language across the Empire with a synchronisation that today's politicians might envy. British governors and their district officers spoke to their ruling partners – African or Pacific Island chiefs, Gulf sheikhs, Indian princes or Chinese community leaders – and the people over whom they ruled, in terms of imperial community, shared identity, common danger and universal duty to the King.

Many people might well have asked "why us?", or expressed bewilderment or disinterest in a white man's war in distant lands. But belonging to an Empire meant that people were subject to powerful global pulses that would bring the war to them even if they did not go to the war. This might take the form of a sudden collapse of the economy, as ships failed to appear to load the export crop massing at the docks. Or, it might mean the bottom falling out of an important branch of the economy, a fate that befell the Gold Coast's cocoa market when trade with Germany ceased. For other colonies, such as Trinidad, the reverse was the case, as the war stoked an insatiable demand for its oil output.

Under attack

War might also come to an imperial outpost in the form of enemy invasion or naval bombardment. In September 1914, the tropical peace of Fanning Island, a coral atoll in the middle of the Pacific, was shattered by the German cruiser *Nürnberg*, which landed a raiding party to destroy the telegraph instruments and cut the submarine cable that made Fanning a link in the all-red cable route encircling the globe.

The First World War showed the Empire's capacity to mobilise people on a scale never before witnessed. Ghanaians invaded German Togoland, West Indians crossed the border from Sierra Leone into German Cameroons, and Jews from soon-to-be-British Palestine formed battalions for the City of London Regiment. Major Hall Brown led 236 men of the Ceylon Planters Rifle Corps to Egypt, where they helped guard the Suez Canal. They were subsequently attached to the Australia and New Zealand Army Corps at Anzac Cove, Gallipoli, where they provided guards for the headquarters staff of the GOC, Lieutenant-General William Birdwood.

The war also brought labourers from all corners of the world to support British battlefronts. Egyptians were recruited in their hundreds of thousands to serve in the Sinai campaign, while an incredible 150,000 Chinese were brought to the Western Front, along with smaller contingents from South Africa, Basutoland, Bechuanaland and Swaziland.

At sea, the Germans attempted to destroy the global movement of

▲ A sailor surveys the wreckage of the SMS *Emden* after her battle with HMAS *Sydney* in November 1914

merchantmen on which the Empire depended for its food and its livelihood, and to terrorise the sea lanes upon which secure imperial communications and the transit of troops rested. This required the Royal Navy to relearn the art of convoy, which had last been employed during the Napoleonic Wars. Enemy commerce raiding disrupted imperial trade, leaving Britain short of vital imports and wreaking havoc on colonial economies that depended upon exports. In attempting to preserve its dominance of the trade routes, Britain fulfilled an important mission on behalf of the Germans by committing fighting resources that might otherwise have been deployed in Europe.

The cruise of the SMS *Emden* in late 1914 provides an excellent example of the threat that a solitary surface raider could pose. Detached from the German Pacific Squadron and sent into the Indian Ocean to harry shipping lanes to the Gulf, India and the Far East, in her brief but swashbuckling career the light cruiser tied down dozens of Allied warships as she captured and sank merchant vessels with abandon.

Sheer audacity

The *Emden* shelled the storage tanks of the Burmah Oil Company at Madras, used Ceylon's own searchlights to target shipping off the port of Colombo and destroyed French and Russian warships in the British harbour of Penang. She also audaciously landed on the British island of Diego Garcia before the inhabitants were aware that war had broken out. However, while raiding the British Cocos-Keeling Islands towards the west coast of Australia, the *Emden*'s luck ran out and HMAS *Sydney* destroyed her.

Africa too saw intriguing naval battles. Off the Swahili coast, the *Königsberg* sank HMS *Pegasus* in Zanzibar harbour before being run to ground in the Rufiji Delta by specially commissioned shallow draft gunboats, sent out from Britain.

Full scale naval actions also took place in imperial settings, such as the Battle of Coronel in the Pacific and the Battle of the Falklands in the South Atlantic.

Indian military engineers laying telephone cables in a trench in Mesopotamia, 1917

In the first encounter, the Germans sank the cruisers HMS *Monmouth* and *Good Hope* with all hands lost, though in the latter clash over 2,000 Germans perished when Vice-Admiral Graf von Spee's powerful squadron was all but annihilated by Vice-Admiral Sir Doveton Sturdee's battle cruiser force on 8 December 1914.

This battle sealed the fate of the German Pacific Squadron and secured control of the ocean trade routes for the British, who relied upon the Anglo-Japanese alliance to police the waters east of the Straits of Malacca.

Projectors of power

The territories of the British Empire were used throughout the war as bases from which to project power and to provide refuelling and resupply facilities essential to a global naval and merchant fleet comprising thousands of vessels.

Falklanders, for example, felt the impact of war on their day-to-day lives every bit as much as their counterparts in Britain. For not only were the islands used by Admiral Sturdee's battle cruisers while hunting for von Spee, men were drafted into the Falkland Islands Volunteer Force, women and children evacuated to inland farms, a minefield was laid and telephone communications established between the warships and observation posts on the hills around Stanley.

By 1914, other overseas shore bases included HMS *Cormorant* at Gibraltar, headquarters of the East Atlantic Station, HMS *St Angelo* in Malta and HMS *Alert* in the Persian Gulf. HMS *Tamar* in Hong Kong was headquarters of the navy's China Station and the North America and West Indies Station was served by HMS *Terror* in Bermuda, which helped police a region in which British ships required protection from the menace of German submarines.

After the Armistice, many British ex-servicemen chose to leave Blighty and make a new start in the colonies of Australia, Canada, Kenya and Southern Rhodesia. However, the Empire was to make one last, and terrible, sacrifice as Spanish influenza stalked demobilised soldiers to their home towns and villages via troopships and railway lines. Around 17 million Indians perished and Samoa lost 25 per cent of its population. It was to prove a tragic twist in the tail of a truly global conflict. **H**

Ashley Jackson is Professor of Imperial and Military History at King's College, London

FURTHER READING

▶ *The Great War: An Imperial History*
by John Morrow (Routledge, 2003)

▶ *The First World War in Africa*
by Hew Strachan (OUP, 2004)

Sex and the trenches

The testimonies of brothel-visiting Tommies offer a poignant insight into how soldiers reacted when stalked by death. **Clare Makepeace** explains

ILLUSTRATION BY FEMKE DE JONG

"**K**eep constantly on your guard against any excesses. In this new experience you may find temptations both in wine and women. You must entirely resist both."

These were the words sent by Lord Kitchener, Britain's Secretary of State for War, to each fighting man in the British Expeditionary Force before they disembarked for the trenches in France during the First World War. But Kitchener's warning received short shrift from some of his men. Among them was Private Richards, who declared that Kitchener's edict "may as well have not been issued for all the notice we took".

One of the temptations that Kitchener had in mind was the legalised brothel, or *maison tolérée*. British soldiers were free to visit these establishments in France for most of the war and one report recorded that 171,000 men

attended brothels in just a single street over the course of a year.

Revealing details
Only a few soldiers wrote about their sexual experiences, but their observations, some of which are now held at the Imperial War Museum in London, provide us with a more complete picture of the Tommy's life. They also add poignancy as to how men reacted when faced with the slaughter of trench warfare.

After arriving in France, Richards visited a brothel, or a 'red lamp' as they were also known, in the village of Béthune. He abstained on this occasion and found his own "respectable bit of goods" in another village. A few days later, he returned. This time there were "300 men in a queue, all waiting their turns to go in the Red Lamp, the majority being mere lads". In 24 hours, these 'lads'

would be fighting in the major British offensive of the Battle of Loos.

Queues were a common sight at any brothel entrance. But they were more than just a way of ensuring men waited their turn; they were also a place for male bonding. Corporal Wood compared the scene outside one red lamp with "a football final in Blighty". Private Amatt recalls the scene inside the brothel: "There was about a dozen girls in there with hardly anything on and high heeled shoes. And they had little what they called chemises then. And they were sitting about on the troops' knees in all sorts of places ... The idea was that if you fancied any girl, you bought her a drink and then took her upstairs."

These were places where, according to Lieutenant Wheatley, men who "might well be dead within a week" could have "a little fun". Lieutenant Butlin found Rouen had been "ruinous" to both his purse and morals, but "from what I heard out here I decided quickly that life must be enjoyed to the full".

Threat of infection

Many had never before experienced sex. Captain Graves observed how "they stood a good chance of being killed within a few weeks… They did not want to die virgins." With so many Tommies frequenting red lamps, it's perhaps hardly surprising that venereal disease was rife among the British army, resulting in 150,000 admissions to hospital in France during the war.

Only in November 1918 were bottles of potassium permanganate lotion and tubes of calomel cream given to soldiers stationed overseas to use for self-disinfection. Before then, they had to trust the measures employed at the brothel, including the "old lady cock examiner", as Private Roworth described her, who checked

each man. The army also advised men to attend their unit's disinfecting stations after brothel visits.

Some soldiers had little interest in such precautions. They frequented brothels because they wanted to catch syphilis or gonorrhea – and, in doing so, secure a more permanent removal from the conflict. At this time, VD was still heavily stigmatised,

> ## "They stood a good chance of being killed within a few weeks... They did not want to die virgins"

and the available treatments for syphilis were dangerous and only partially effective. But they did entail about one month's stay in hospital – a worthwhile trade-off for some, if it enabled them to escape the carnage of the front line.

Having regular sex in brothels was believed, by others, to be imperative for their health. As Lieutenant Dixon wrote: "We were not monks, but fighting soldiers certainly with an abundance of physical energy… and if bought love is no substitute for the real thing, it at any rate seemed better than nothing." This belief was so widespread that a member of parliament impressed on the officers "that continence is neither impossible nor harmful".

This thinking led to the perverse idea that it was more acceptable for married men, rather than single men, to visit prostitutes. Lance Corporal Chaney, while he surveyed a queue of soldiers outside one red lamp, was told these places "were not for young lads like me, but for married men who were missing their wives". Private Clare also remembered a chaplain who excused unfaithfulness to spouses under the present circumstances, but advised the men to only use licensed brothels, otherwise they might contract disease.

When the war ended, men declared their readiness to return to their marital beds. For Dixon "the business was compartmentalised". His "sweet-heart in Blighty" did not belong to the "topsy-turvy world of the battle-fronts, where values were totally different". The red lamps that had "amused and disgusted" Private Holt as he was redeployed across France "faded away completely when [he] left the towns".

Whether this really was the end of their indulgences, we do not know, since their descriptions stop with the armistice. As the combination of officially accessible brothels, an all-male environment and the conditions of battle faded, so too does this rare glimpse into men's commercial sexual indulgence. **H**

Clare Makepeace is currently studying for a PhD on the lives of British prisoners of war during the Second World War

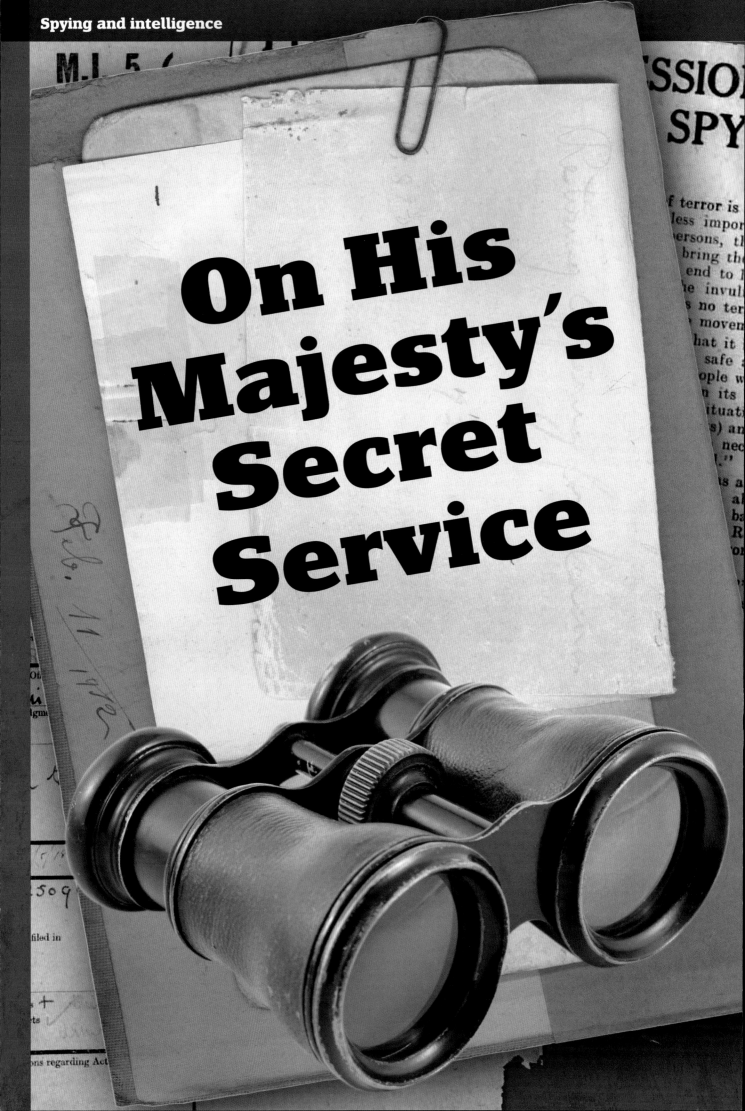

On His Majesty's Secret Service

A century ago, the War Office created a shadowy organisation whose remit was to snare enemy spies in Britain and plant secret agents abroad. **Michael S Goodman** tells the story of the Secret Service Bureau's clandestine war with Germany

The journalist Valentine Williams, who served as a secret agent in the First World War, once wrote: "Through many books on secret service published in England since the war, a shadowy figure goes gliding. A man of power and mystery looms up, the guiding hand behind our secret service...I used to go and chat with him at his wartime headquarters situated in the attics of a block of residential flats near Charing Cross. A private lift shot the caller up seven floors to a regular maze of passages, steps, and oddly shaped rooms." Another wartime spy recalled that "I do not know to this day who he is. He is simply known as 'C'".

Sir Mansfield Cumming (aka 'C') was a spymaster like no other. In October 1909, having accepted the offer to head up the foreign branch of the Secret Service Bureau (SSB) and operating out of a small flat in central London, Cumming would create MI6, an organisation unparalleled in mystique and secrecy.

The Secret Service Bureau was not the first British intelligence organisation – in one form or another, there had existed such a system for nearly 400 years, stretching back to the time of Elizabeth I. Yet the SSB was different: it operated in a new way and had a specific threat to guard against. The result was that the security of the United Kingdom was left to two individuals: one, Cumming, a retired naval commander; the other, army captain Vernon Kell, Cumming's counterpart for domestic intelligence.

A clear enemy
What was the threat? In simple terms – and known to the government and public alike – it was the danger posed by Germany. This fear was fuelled by William Le Queux, a very popular and prolific writer of the day who, in 1906, published a book called *The Invasion Of 1910*. Although a rather fanciful account of the German invasion of Britain, it became an overnight success and was followed by several other books that described the dastardly Germans and their plots to invade and take over the country.

Despite the obvious point that these were imaginary accounts, before long,

fact and fiction became indistinguishable. From that point onwards, British intelligence developed a shadowy, mysterious demeanour.

The effect of Le Queux's books was to create mass hysteria. Members of the public began to contact the government about strange gentlemen seen wandering around the country with maps, speaking in foreign languages. By 1908, this had reached a crescendo.

While interviewing, C would stab a letter opener into his wooden leg to gauge a potential recruit's reaction

Many within the government believed the hype generated by these fictitious accounts and the head of military intelligence in the War Office decided something ought to be done. Since the late 1800s, a small 'Secret Service Branch' had existed, headed by an Irish resident magistrate – essentially a law enforcement outfit designed to deal with the threat posed by Irish terrorists. The military intelligence supremo now produced a note on the need to create a new secret service, one focused on Germany and based on the reporting and running of secret agents. The backbone of this was a very real fear about what would happen if nothing were done: "unless a secret service system is prepared, we shall enter a war fatally handicapped".

By January 1909, this had reached the highest echelons of the military. War with Germany was no longer considered a matter of 'if', but 'when'. They considered it to be of "sufficient importance and interest" that it be passed to the Committee of Imperial Defence, at that time the most senior meeting of officials, chaired by the Prime Minister and designed to look at future defence issues.

▲ Sir Mansfield Cumming created MI6 after sea-sickness forced him out of the navy

In turn, they convened a special group to look at this matter. Of particular importance to them was how other countries had approached the creation of a secret service. Frederick the Great, the legendary Prussian king who had embraced an intelligence system, was recorded as having said to his generals, "When Marshal Soubise [his French enemy whom he defeated in 1757] goes on service, he has a hundred cooks following him. When I go, I send a hundred spies ahead of me".

▷

IMPERIAL WAR MUSEUM, DREAMSTIME, THINKSTOCK

▷ Of course, the basis for any secret service is that it remains secret. Even by 1890, in some instructions by the then head of the 'Secret Service Branch', it was observed that "if questions are asked in the House [of Commons] … I hope you will keep my name from the public, any success I have had has been largely owing to the fact that my name has never come out".

By mid-1909, the special sub-committee concluded that Britain did indeed need a secret service, not least because they regarded "with apprehension the increasing amount of German espionage that is taking place in this country". As evidence, they cited 47 instances of such espionage in 1908, with a further 24 cases reported in the first three months of 1909 alone. We now know that these figures were hugely exaggerated and, although there

was some limited German espionage in England, it was far less prevalent than the statistics suggested.

Dual function

The response was to propose the creation of a 'Secret Service Bureau' with dual functions: monitoring the German threat at home, while gathering intelligence abroad about German military developments. The government approved these plans and measures were taken to locate suitable candidates to head the two branches. These were found and, in October 1909, the Secret Service Bureau began its operations. The two chiefs were dynamic figures, known by their *nom du guerres* of 'K' and 'C'.

Britain's modern intelligence community began life modestly. Initially based in the same office, Cumming and Captain Vernon Kell (aka K) faced the daunting task of creating an intelligence system by themselves, with only the assistance of a shared clerk. Money was a constant problem and, when he decided to move out and have his own office, Cumming personally contributed the rent for his new premises. There is some debate as to how well the two spymasters got on – and it is certainly not clear from the records. What is obvious is how different their personalities and backgrounds were.

K, the War Office representative, came from a well-to-do family. He had spent a considerable amount of time abroad, was cultured and well versed

in foreign languages, speaking French, German, Russian and Chinese.

By contrast, C had a more modest upbringing, enrolling in the navy at an early age. Having spent time on various ships, Cumming, rather sadly for a sailor, began to suffer from severe sea-sickness, to the extent that he could no longer spend extended time on the seas. He moved to Southampton and spent a decade working on boom defences, essentially a chain of timber lengths stretched from one side of the harbour to the other, designed to stop a ship passing through. C spoke French and, with the threat coming from Germany, taught himself that language too. He was obsessed with what we might now describe as gadgets, being one of the first aeroplane enthusiasts and regularly racing motorcars.

Looking back now, it seems odd that K was chosen for the domestic service and C for the foreign branch. Of the two, C was the more dynamic and certainly the more eccentric. During the war, he went to visit his son in France and, speeding back to base, his car overturned, trapping him by his leg underneath. His son was thrown out and knocked unconscious. Seeing that his help was needed, rumour has it that C took out his penknife and hacked his own leg off. Alas, his efforts were in vain; his son died. Despite a short convalescence, C was back at work in no time, having had a wooden prosthetic leg fitted.

While interviewing potential recruits, C would often stab a letter opener into his wooden leg, concealed as normal beneath his trousers, while gauging the applicant's reaction to test their suitability. He was also known for racing around the corridors of government departments on an electric scooter, as well as being famed for not starting meetings until he had finished his cup of tea – surely one of life's better lessons!

Within a month of the Secret Service Bureau's creation, C was given permission to move out and take up his own flat. This split marked, in essence, the separation of the Secret Service Bureau into two separate organisations. Kell's half would become MI5, the fifth branch of military intelligence, responsible for counter-espionage and domestic intelligence. Cumming's part would initially be known as MI1c, part of the MI1 military intelligence branch of the War Office.

Initially, the all-pervading aura of secrecy had a limiting role on their performance. Situated opposite the army and navy stores, where both were well

IMPERIAL WAR MUSEUM, GETTY, DREAMSTIME X2, LIBRARY OF CONGRESS

▲ Sir Mansfield Cumming, or 'C', head of the SSB's foreign branch, is said to have hacked his own leg off with a penknife in a bid to save his son's life

SECRET

Early Secret Service Dossier

- In the first six months of its existence, Kell's domestic branch investigated over 200 cases of alleged espionage, creating a database of over 500 'aliens'.

- By the start of the war, C had created a European network of agents, with the major base being in Brussels.

- The first foreign spy to be tried was Siegfried Helm, a German soldier seen wandering around the south coast of England.

- Some of the first German 'spies' did not try to conceal themselves: Dr Max Schultz, for instance, was arrested after flying a German flag from his houseboat near Plymouth.

- The only pre-war trial to involve a Briton alleged to have been involved in espionage was the case of George Parrott, a warrant officer in the Royal Navy who was "entrapped by a woman".

- One of the most successful espionage networks was La Dame Blanche (the White Lady), a system of trainspotters during the war who recorded the movement of German locomotives.

- One of MI6's agents, Paul Dukes, was knighted for his espionage activities in Russia.

- The most notorious British spy was Sidney Reilly, an agent who spent much of his time in Russia and was allegedly executed by the Bolsheviks after being caught plotting against them.

- By December 1914, the headquarters of MI6 had just four officers, four clerks, two typists, one messenger, and two 'outside men'.

- Cumming stayed in post for 14 years, until his death in 1923, while Kell remained in his for 31 years, until he was removed in 1940. Both are the longest serving heads of MI6 and MI5 respectively.

▲ Paul Dukes joined the Soviet secret police and the Red Army while employed by MI6

There was an all-pervading aura of secrecy. They could only meet an agent at an anonymous address

known, neither officer was allowed to be seen by anyone they knew, could not talk about their present work and, if they were to meet an agent, it had to be at an anonymous address. The frequent result, as C recorded in his diary, was one of solitude and desperation: "office all day – no-one appeared".

Cash for questions

Money, too, continued to play a significant role, not just in the ability to have a permanent staff, but also to pay for informants. While it was recognised that patriotic Britons would help K's task, for C to succeed he had to have enough money to compensate agents and to pay for the transmission of their information back to London.

One example of the paranoia pervading Britain in those pre-war years – and of how the system of snaring German spies often worked in practice – is provided by the 'Rusper case'. In a report on the first six months with the SSB, K provided further details.

A patriotic Briton, a "lady of high social standing", was in her local post office when she overheard "two foreigners (Herr A and Herr B) having a discussion about a foreign money-order, which they were wanting to cash.

"Being herself a good linguist, she offered to assist them. In doing so, this lady noticed that the money-order was made payable to a Polish-German name … her interest and suspicions were roused, and after making some enquiries in the neighbourhood, ▷

▶ Vernon Kell, or 'K', was head of the nascent MI5. He was tasked with crushing the threat posed by German spies in Britain Army while employed by MI6

THE ACE OF SPIES

Security service files on the British agent Sidney Reilly

These British secret service files, released by the National Archives in 2002, relate to the British agent Sidney Reilly. It's claimed Reilly worked behind German lines in the First World War and took part in a plot to overthrow the Bolshevik government, before being shot by Soviet agents in 1925. Reilly has since gained fame as the 'ace of spies', the subject of a 1983 TV series. The documents here include a photo of him, a newspaper article following his death and a letter from his wife, Pepita Haddon Chambers, to Mansfield Cumming.

M.I. 5 (G.) I.P. No. 279105

I.P. Form 14c.

(4.4.19) W5751—26 50,000 3/18 HWV.(P1582)

CONFIDENTIAL: NOT TO

OUT FOR INDEXING IMMEDIATE

Date of Receipt	From			
30.4.18	To	M.I.c.		
Sender's Date	Sender's Reference No.		Enclosure
29.4.18	BM.	Cx 029028	

Subjects

No enquiries necessary
re telegram from —
k —

Names

REILLY

LITVINOFF] doubt

Referred and Date

Former Papers

Minutes

INTERNAL MEMORAND...

From London Region .... To R 3 B.

Mrs. Pepita BOBADILLA @ HADDON CHAMBERS
L.183A/83.

Reference our telephone conversation this morning.

I obtained W.E.'s permission for the papers in their held L.183A/83 to be incorporated in P.F.25096 for Sidney George REILLY, and thus should be grateful if this could be done and, of course, W.E. notified.

Date.....29.11.44..

Catalogue Reference:kv/

FURTHER CONFESSIONS OF REILLY THE SPY

WHY did Sidney Reilly, the British spy, re-enter Soviet Russia (with a forged passport) in September, 1925?

Was it to test his "new ideas" about the possibility of "peaceful co-operation" with the Soviet Government, which according to Reilly's confession (printed last week) he conceived in 1922?

Not at all. Reilly says: "I entered Soviet Russia on my own initiative, because I heard of the existence of an apparently serious anti-Soviet group in the Soviet Union."

A little later, however, Reilly let the cat out of the bag. "Before my departure I had talks with many persons, belonging to quarters influential in Russian affairs, in London and America.'" And in a further statement, which Reilly described as "perfectly frank," he added: "I talked about my journey with Churchill...."

"If I had returned, I should have communicated my impressions as to the extent to which the group previously mentioned might represent a serious factor in the anti-Bolshevik movement.

"and to what extent it deserves political and financial support."

But was this the only purpose of Reilly's visit? It is the only one mentioned in his confession. But is...

"The aim of terror is always a double one. The first and less important is the removal of dangerous persons, the second and more important is to bring the morass into movement, to put an end to lethargy, to destroy the legend of the invulnerability of authority. If there is no terror it means there is no spirit in the movement.

"You may say that it is easy to speak of terror when one is safe abroad, but I tell you that I know people who have expended tremendous energy in its preparation (suitable to the present situation and the latest technical improvements) and are prepared to begin immediately the necessary means are placed at their disposal."

British Labour now has a chance of weighing up Tory hypocrisy about "Bolshevik savagery" and "Asiatic barbarism" at its true value. Further on, Reilly proceeds to give a sketch of the terrorist organisation as he sees it.

"Such an organisation," writes Reilly, "requires an exceptionally strong conspirative centre. Whether this can exist for any length of time in the present circumstances I don't know."

Terrorism, lying, organisation, insurrecti...

37 BEAUCHAMP PLACE
S.W. 3

Kensington 0300

Dear Mr. "Mansfield"
It has been reported to me that a man called "Simonovitch" has been seen in London — Can you verify this? Simonovitch is the next...

BRUXELLES
1931

Intelligence Service

Londres

Angleterre.

Catalogue Reference:kv/2/827

▷ she discovered that these two foreigners were living a few miles from her place; also that they had no visible occupation."

The lady's report was passed to the SSB to investigate. It was discovered that both men regularly travelled around the Sussex/Surrey region. Although not explicitly mentioned, it is clear that both were thought to be German spies.

Despite all the difficulties encountered in the first years in their new roles, the humble start – not to mention the uphill challenge they faced – both K and C had a measure of success. As the saying goes, money certainly talked. Both MI5 and the infant MI6 were able to recruit a range of spies, at home and abroad, and this network ensured that, when war did start in 1914, both could argue that they were prepared for it.

Within the UK, Kell boasted about the number of spies he had rounded up. He certainly met with some success for, by October 1914, the home secretary could claim that German espionage had been "crushed at the outbreak of war". C had fewer triumphs to report, though arguably his task was far harder. Both had a 'good war' and emerged victorious. Perhaps the greatest example of their successes is the fact that they, and their agencies, survived.

'Intelligence', as it would have been understood in the first decade of the SSB's existence, is different to how it is perceived today. Back then, it was a purely military discipline, both in terms of its personnel and its targets. Both C and K were concerned exclusively with capabilities – gathering information on, for instance, German shipyards, weapons, and locations of spies in the UK.

C called his agents as 'scallywags'. For them, it was all about pure, hard money

There was no real attempt to try to understand German intentions – when she might launch war, where and why. This was a reflection of the military environment in which the agencies worked and of the interests of the people who worked in them.

'Intelligence' was also different in the way it was conducted. The primary source of information was through agents, men who 'volunteered' their services in exchange for cash. There is very little evidence of the ideological motivation that would characterise the inter-war period – it was all about pure, hard money. Perhaps it is for this very reason that C referred to his agents as 'scallywags'.

Modern intelligence is a far more varied affair. The range of topics are broader, as are the methods of gathering information. The system is also much larger. Yet there are still similarities between 1909 and today. Money will always play a central role in the affairs of state, while the role of the spy – the agent on the ground – has never been more crucial.

British intelligence has had mixed fortunes, but, at the very least, its pioneering creation five years before the outbreak of the First World War meant that Britain was prepared, and had set in place a secret service that was to endure.

C and K would probably be shocked to see how their two-man enterprise has transformed more than 100 years later, but they would surely be pleased. C in particular would look back with a wry smile on his face, to see just how prophetic their actions of 1909 had been. ⌂

Michael S Goodman is a senior lecturer in the Department of War Studies at King's College London and a regular contributor to *BBC History Magazine*

FACING NEW THREATS The secret service from 1918 to today

The war's end saw a great reappraisal of the scope and remit of the intelligence services, for which, in 1919, the **Secret Service Committee was created**.

The German threat had been defeated, but in its place was a better organised and more menacing foe – **the Soviet Union**. Bolshevism had triumphed with the 1917 revolution and the Secret Intelligence Service (SIS, known as MI6) lost no time in trying to infiltrate agents and spies in an attempt to see what was going on.

The changing threat was also reflected, subtly at first, by a changing definition of intelligence. Although still military in content, 'intelligence' began to get more involved in political

matters: at home, a growing concern in the 1920s was **Soviet involvement in workers' strikes**.

Not everyone thought that the intelligence services were a good thing. **The highest profile opponent was the Foreign Office**, which disliked MI6 for two reasons: first, that espionage was seen as ungentlemanly; second, that agents abroad were attached to British military missions undermined the gentle efforts of the Foreign Office.

These views only began to change in the late 1930s with a **resurgence of the German threat**. By the outbreak of war in 1939, MI5 and MI6 had been complemented by the **Joint Intelligence Committee**, a body designed to stream-line British intelligence in an attempt to avoid duplicating effort.

The General Strike of 1926. The secret service feared Soviet involvement in industrial action

Britain's intelligence services again had a good war and **the agencies continued to flourish** – largely because the foreign threat seemed so real. **The Soviet Union once more became public enemy number one** and it remained the core function of British intelligence. With the collapse of the Soviet bloc and **the end of the Cold War,** many people thought that

the intelligence agencies had been proved victorious and were no longer needed.

But today the work of the intelligence agencies is in the public sphere like never before. Intelligence is no longer the missing dimension of governmental work, yet its work remains as crucial now as it did 100 years ago.

MIRRORPIX, THE NATIONAL ARCHIVES X5

GALLIPOLI
WHAT WENT WRONG?

Peter Hart, author of an important study of this disastrous First World War campaign in 1915, offers his explanations for the Allies' bloody failure

The Gallipoli campaign was a terrible tragedy. The attempt by the Allies to seize the Gallipoli peninsula (now part of modern-day Turkey) from the Ottoman Empire and gain control over the strategically important Dardanelles failed in a welter of hubris, blood and suffering. Located just across the Dardanelles straits from the fabled city of Troy, its classical undertones have helped create a rich mythology of 'the terrible ifs'; of what might have been achieved with 'a bit more luck'.

The beach landings at Helles – the first made against modern weapons systems – saw incredible heroism and turned the sea at V Beach red with blood.

Gallipoli is today synonymous with the achievement of the Australian and New Zealander Army Corps (ANZAC) in carving out a small bridgehead at Anzac Cove. That maze of tangled gullies and ridges is still sacred for Australians. But for all that the campaign was an utter failure. The question is why? ◼

Peter Hart is a military historian specialising in the First World War. He is the author of *Gallipoli* (Profile, 2011)

---

1 POORLY CONCEIVED

When the Ottoman Turks attacked Russians in the Caucasus mountains in December 1914, Russia asked her allies for help. A group of politicians led by Winston Churchill sought to help Russia with an attack on the Gallipoli peninsula that aimed to gain control of the Dardanelles straits that separated Asia and Europe. This, it was boasted, would remove one of the allies 'propping up' Germany and open the sea route for the export of munitions to feed Russian guns on the Eastern Front.

Much of this was nonsense. There was no backdoor to Germany; no easy route to victory, no allies that propped her up. Germany operated on interior lines of communications and even in the event of a Turkish defeat would merely have rushed reinforcements to bolster her Austro-Hungarian allies.

Finally, Britain did not have sufficient munitions for her own armies and was forced to fight the war as it was, not how visionaries dreamt it might be. The priority of the Western Front meant that the Gallipoli expedition could never be given sufficient men and guns to have any chance of success. As such, it should never have been started.

▶ An Australian carries a wounded comrade back for medical attention

British soldiers make bombs from empty jam tins at Helles in June 1915

2 IT WAS 1915

The British Army of 1915 wasn't ready for war. There were not enough guns or shells for the Gallipoli campaign to have any chance against Turkish troops once they were well dug in. Success demanded hundreds of guns that didn't exist, fired by gunners not yet trained, using complex artillery techniques that had not been invented, firing hundreds of thousands of shells as yet not manufactured. It required infantry tactics not yet painfully developed in the heat of battle and support weapons not yet imagined.

The Gallipoli campaign suffered in many ways: a lack of realistic goals; no coherent plan; the use of inexperienced troops for whom this would be the first campaign; a failure to comprehend or properly disseminate maps and intelligence; negligible artillery support; totally inadequate logistical and medical arrangements; a gross underestimation of the enemy; and incompetent local commanders – all overlaid with lashings of misplaced over-confidence.

3 INFERIOR LEADERSHIP

The British commander was General Sir Ian Hamilton, one of Britain's greatest soldiers. He was no fool, but his plans for Gallipoli were fatally over-complicated. He launched multiple attacks, each dependent on each other's success, but was left isolated when things went wrong. Taken as a whole, his schemes were utterly unrealistic. Everything had to go right, but his plans demanded incredible feats of heroism; raw troops would have to perform like veterans and incompetent subordinates lead like Napoleons. Above all, his plans demanded that the Turks put up little resistance. When the landings failed, he blamed everyone but himself:

"Behind us we had a swarm of adverse influences: our own General Headquarters in France, the chief of the imperial general staff of the War Office, the first sea lord of the Admiralty, the French cabinet and the best organised part of the British press. Fate willed it so. Faint hearts and feeble wills seemed for a while to succeed in making vain the sacrifices of Anzac, Helles and Suvla. Only the dead men stuck it out to the last."

Opposing Hamilton was a German, General Otto Liman von Sanders. A steady professional, Liman husbanded his reserves until he knew what the British were doing before committing them to devastating effect. He was fortunate indeed in one of his Turkish subordinates – Colonel Mustafa Kemal. As Kemal led his 57th Regiment into action against the Anzacs on 25 April, his chilling words have gone down in legend:

"I don't order you to attack – I order you to die. In the time which passes until we die, other troops and commanders can take our places." This unflinching martial spirit inspired the Turkish troops to victory.

▲ British commander General Sir Ian Hamilton. He was overshadowed by his opposite number, Otto Liman von Sanders

---

4 THE TURKS

Colonel Mustafa Kemal, who became President Kemal Atatürk after the war, summed up the grit and determination demonstrated by his countrymen at Gallipoli. A good proportion of the Turkish soldiers had recent experience fighting in the Balkan wars of 1912-13, but all of them came from a country where life was hard. They made tough, well-disciplined soldiers when fighting in defence of their homeland.

"Our officers and soldiers who with love for their motherland and religion and heroism protected the doors of their capital Constantinople against such a strong enemy, won the right to a status which we can be proud of," he announced. "I congratulate all the members of the fighting units under my command. I remember with deep and eternal respect, all the ones who sacrificed their lives and became martyrs for this great objective."

In contrast, most of the Allied troops committed to battle were inadequately trained. It wasn't that they weren't keen, it was just that they were not yet ready for war in such an unforgiving environment as Gallipoli. The Turks were experienced and well led. They were determined to win – and they did.

Turkish troops on parade during the First World War, led by Kemal Atatürk (inset)

Making do: an improvised British harbour made out of grounded ships

5 LOGISTICS

The United Kingdom was some 2,000 miles away and the nearest 'real' base was that of Alexandria back in Egypt, with its spacious quays, cranes, lighters, tugboats and plentiful labour. Yet it was nearly 700 miles from Alexandria to Gallipoli. The advanced base of Mudros on the island of Lemnos, some 60 miles from Helles, had a good natural anchorage, but that was all it offered – there were no port facilities. A phenomenal amount of work was required to build it up into a military supply base.

There was an advanced supply depot at Imbros, but even then there were still 15 miles of open sea to the Gallipoli peninsula where all the thousands of tonnes of necessary foodstuffs and munitions had to be landed on open beaches. Makeshift piers were all they had and these were ephemeral in the face of the raw power of the sea. Turkish shells crashed down on the beaches every day of the campaign, while soon U-boats lurked offshore.

Gallipoli was a logistical nightmare that would make any responsible staff officer tear his hair out. As a method of waging warfare, it was insanity.

Read more from Peter Hart on the Gallipoli campaign on the BBC website ➜ bbc.in/OVKeOG

··· PART TWO ···
THE STORY OF THE WAR

The battles intensify, as **Peter Caddick-Adams** continues his analysis
of the 50 key elements that shaped the Great War

Medics move among the dead and
wounded on the beach at Anzac Cove
on the day of the landing

GETTY X2, MARY EVANS PICTURE LIBRARY

16 GALLIPOLI

As First Lord Of The Admiralty, Winston Churchill was keen to dominate the Turkish-held Dardenelles and develop a sea route to reach Britain's ally, Russia. But his attempts at achieving this through naval warfare came unstuck on 18 March 1915, when British and French warships were sunk or damaged by mines.

The local commanders then advised landing troops on the rugged Gallipoli Peninsula. But assembling the men – from Britain, India and the Australian and New Zealand Army Corps (ANZAC) – required six weeks. This time-lapse allowed Turkish forces in the area, two divisions under then unknown Colonel Mustafa Kemal (later Atatürk), to prepare.

On 25 April, British and French troops landed around the tip of Cape Helles, while the ANZACs hit the Aegean coast at a small inlet they called Anzac Cove. On two beaches, the attackers suffered 70 per cent casualties but, once ashore, some managed to advance inland.

The ANZACs were more adventurous until meeting Turkish counter attacks, which almost drove them back into the sea. The Allies clung on through May to July in torrid heat, plagued by dysentery and typhoid, but both sides had fought to a standstill.

After reinforcement, on 6-7 August, the ANZACs broke out north towards the high ground of Chunuk Bair, but were beaten back by Kemal. Other Australians seized the Ottoman trenches at Lone Pine.

Simultaneously, the British landed at Suvla, but Kemal was quick to seize the dominating ground. Stalemate again. A new commander, Sir Charles Monro, advised withdrawal and, after much anguish, London agreed. The Allied evacuation of December and January was the best-run part of the operation, with not a single man being lost.

Gallipoli cost the Allies 250,000 casualties, of whom 27,000 were French and 35,000 ANZACs. The Turkish experience is only now beginning to be understood, with its 250,000 casualties, but the campaign has been claimed, with every justification, as their own by Australia and New Zealand.

▶▶▶ GALLIPOLI – PAGE 40

17 THE MILITARY BECOMES PROFESSIONAL

The German war machine comprised a vast conscript army, permanently on the defensive, being sandwiched between two potentially aggressive rivals – France and Russia. The rationale of how to manoeuvre the huge force to oppose either one or both neighbours led to the birth of the Prussian General Staff in 1814, towards the end of the Napoleonic era.

To maximise effectiveness, officers were taught how to plan large-scale campaigns, and rehearse them during peacetime. Mock battles and manoeuvres were fought, tactics considered, and military history closely studied in situ. German success in the Franco-Prussian War of 1870-1 was largely ascribed to the excellence of its staff work, where all the planners had been trained through their staff college (the Berlin Kriegsakademie) to think and speak as one. In war, the role of German staff officers was also to advise their commanders, even deputising for them. They came to be seen as the elite of their army.

Consequently, a British staff college was founded at Camberley in 1858. However, attendance on the two-year course was not, initially, deemed necessary for a successful career. The course produced 60 graduates a year – woefully inadequate to administer a British army that peaked at nearly three million on the Western Front in 1917. However, Camberley closed in August 1914, and half its talented graduates soon became casualties serving with their regiments in the first few months of fighting.

A contributory factor to lacklustre generalship in 1914-7 was the lack of good staff officers – many performing the role with no staff training at all. Eventually, staff schools were opened in France and at Cambridge to correct this deficiency. Battlefield performance improved as staff learned to coordinate the army's assets (engineers, artillery, aircraft, tanks) at high levels, rather than expend them in penny packets (small units). A gulf grew between

▲ Camberley Staff College, which produced a mere 60 graduates a year, was closed in 1914

staff officers, distinguished by armbands and red cloth gorgets worn on the collar, and their combat counterparts, hence the derisory nickname of the former, 'Bloody Red Tabs'. Yet much of the British success of 1918 must be attributed to the creation of a professional staff system.

18 WEAK BRITISH GENERALS?

No subject provokes more controversy in the 1914-18 war than generalship. The continental armies, because of conscription, were always large and trained talented officers for high command: not so with the smaller BEF.

British First World War generals had no training for their command, other than attendance at Staff College when a captain or major. This was because the small, all-volunteer British force was never expected to grow large, and few would ever control a division, let alone a corps or

army. When the BEF mushroomed overnight, large numbers of senior officers had to be found to run it. For example, 73 infantry and eight cavalry divisions were formed, each requiring a major-general and four brigadiers. Relatively junior competent officers found themselves promoted into positions sometimes beyond their expectations – or competence. As the war ground on, they also had to contend with the arrival of new technologies, making the business of battle incredibly complex.

The statistic that 78 British and Empire Brigadiers-General and above died on active service in the war, while a further 146 were wounded, surprises many, and as a proportion of their numbers, they suffered a higher casualty rate than far more junior subordinates. This shows that British commanders frequently went close enough to the battle zone to place themselves in danger. However, these losses should also never have happened. Whilst they were undoubtedly brave, their training should have prepared them to command at a safer distance. Their job was to oversee and direct operations, not expose themselves to danger.

It is often overlooked that senior commanders were liked and widely respected during the war – Douglas Haig in particular. Many commanders drifted around the front, meeting their men. But the impact and knowledge of this was limited because of the trenches. The question is often asked as to why British generalship was so poor during 1914-18, yet with no school for generals we should perhaps ask how the army managed to become so well led and proficient by 1918.

◄ Many British Generals had little or no suitable training for the war they would encounter

19 THE IMPORTANCE OF MESOPOTAMIA

The discovery of oil in Iraq (then called Mesopotamia) and Persia (now Iran) when the Royal Navy was converting from coal to oil gave the area strategic importance. In November 1914, Allied troops landed to protect the refineries from Turkey, who had joined the Central Powers on 28 October. Moving first to Basra, before dividing at the junction of the Tigris and Euphrates in May 1915, one column, under Major General Charles Townshend advanced up the Tigris towards Baghdad, while a second followed the Euphrates.

As the Ottoman army was trained, equipped and led by the Germans, and Baghdad was the terminus of the Berlin-Baghdad railway, capturing the Mesopotamian capital

became a way of hitting back at Germany when deadlock reigned over the Western Front.

Baghdad became a siren, luring Townsend on and stretching his supply lines. But as his supply lines grew longer, those of the Turks became shorter. His men, unused to the local climate, begun to tire after their long advances, and many succumbed to disease.

In September 1915, they occupied Kut-al-Amara, and by November were 24 miles from Baghdad, where they met strong Turkish resistance. By now, they had pushed their luck too far, and without reserves they fell back to Kut, surrounded.

Meanwhile, the end of the Gallipoli campaign allowed the Turks

to reinforce. After failed relief attempts, Kut, along with 8,000 British troops, fell on 26 April 1916.

Reacting to the humiliation, London reinforced massively, with operations resuming in August 1916. Kut was retaken in February 1917 and Baghdad entered on 11 March, as the Turks weakened. Lieutenant General Maude died of cholera in November 1917, but his forces pushed beyond.

In late October 1918, they seized the wells at Mosul, fighting their last battle near the ancient Assyrian city of Ashur. The campaign, which had begun and ended with the seizure of oilfields, cost the British army 92,000 casualties, including 27,000 fatalities – 13,000 of whom died through disease.

▼ The Indian Expeditionary Force load supplies ahead of the 1915 advance up the Tigris towards Baghdad

20 THE HUGE LOSSES AT VERDUN

Verdun epitomises the carnage of the Great War for France. Lying on the River Meuse, the old Roman settlement, later fortified by 17th-century military engineer Vauban, had been captured in 1870, and became a keystone of the new Franco-German frontier. By 1916, it was a quiet sector, bulging into German lines.

Looking for a breakthrough along the Western Front, Falkenhayn, chief of the German general staff, opted to attack the ring of forts around Verdun, assuming that its prestige to the French would cause them to "throw in every man they have. If they do, the forces of France will bleed to death."

Operation Gericht (Judgment) was launched on 21 February 1916 with a Trommelfeuer (drum fire) bombardment of one million shells. Within days, German stormtroops had reached and taken the ridge crowned by Douaumont, the strongest of Verdun's forts.

Joffre appointed Philippe Pétain, a stolid infantryman, to command the defence. He ended costly counter-attacks, preferring artillery to take the strain. The Bar-le-Duc road became the logistics artery by which Verdun survived. Day and night, men and supplies passed up, the wounded down, giving it the deserved title la Voie Sacrée – the Sacred Way.

Operations lost momentum by March but renewed attacks seized Fort Vaux on 7 June, and in July a final spurt took the Germans to the top of Fort Souville, overlooking Verdun. But they could not continue. After the Somme attack, Falkenhayn was dismissed on 29 August, his attritional strategy discredited. That autumn, the French retook the lost ground, and Douaumont was recaptured on 24 October. The struggle had ended by December, but the ground remained fought over until late 1918, nine villages being obliterated from the map.

We cannot be sure of casualties, but each side lost more than 300,000, with French losses exceeding German. Pétain's slogan 'Ils ne passeront pas' ('They shall not pass') ensured his pre-eminence, which propelled him into an unwise devil's bargain with another generation of Germans in 1940.

▲ French troops prepare for battle in their trench in the countryside of Verdun

German soldiers enjoy a welcome quiet moment in their trench to catch up on mail

21 TRENCH WARFARE

The defining characteristic of 1914-18 was the scale and duration of trench warfare, a consequence of the available manpower and firepower. Trenches were far older than the war. Faced with stalemate, combatants burrowed into their institutional memories and the terminology and techniques of siege warfare reappeared.

They were initially a temporary measure, but all soon realised they allowed a front to be lightly held and reinforcements rushed to critical sectors. However, as a result of Allied offensives in early 1915, the Germans dug a second line that enabled them to repulse the British at Loos in September.

Trenches generally followed a Greek key or zig-zag pattern, to minimise the effect of shell bursts and limit hostile penetrations. Steps led down to numerous subterranean shelters, stores, headquarters and dugouts: most soldiers spent their day underground, unless on sentry duty. Pumps were incorporated to remove flooding, though too often the mud remained. Battalions rotated through the front and rarely spent more than a week there.

Both sides reinforced their lines with strong points, often the brick cellars of old farmhouses, housing multiple machine-guns covering 'No Man's Land'. There was no set distance between the opposing trenches – occasionally a mile, sometimes twenty yards. Wire entanglements in front prevented raiding parties attacking at night.

A soldier traversing his trench was usually safe, but both sides employed snipers to kill the unwary or important-looking visitors – dozens of British generals died this way. Trench periscopes took away some of this risk, but for a clear view, soldiers were obliged to stand on an earthen step – the parapet.

Trench warfare was uncomfortable, boring and often frightening. Soldiers recalled the rats, which fed on corpses and discarded food, the stench of excreta and unwashed bodies, the flies in summer and lice in winter. In wet conditions, troops suffered from 'trench foot', which – in extremis – required amputation.

A variety of ailments went under the name of 'trench fever', which might involve a high temperature, or more unpleasant side effects. Modern researchers are now wondering whether this was the origin of the 1918 influenza epidemic that killed millions.

22 NEW TECHNOLOGY

The war saw the introduction of a huge array of new technologies, but many of these were old ideas reintroduced into the battlespace. It was the ability to integrate military innovation that was important. Machine-guns had already seen nearly 50 years in combat zones before their power was fully concentrated and exploited on the Western Front. Mortars and hand grenades were both old technologies that reappeared as solutions to the proliferation of trench warfare and the need for indirect fire.

Poison gas finds its origins in older forms of chemical and biological warfare where sulphur was used to poison defenders of castles, and where diseased carcasses were catapulted over walls to induce epidemics and spread terror. Even the Ancient Greeks had used fire as a weapon, which reappeared in the German flammenwerfer of 1915.

Tanks originate with Leonardo da Vinci, yet the opportunities to use a 'landship' were limited until the concept of a protected chariot was harnessed to a trench-crossing platform. Initially, they were let down more usually by their primitive engines than hostile fire. The Italians had previously used aircraft in Libya (1912-13), suppressing Arab tribes, whilst HG Wells had hinted as their potential in his pre-war science fiction. A submarine was first used in the US Civil War, but it was Germany's ability to produce enough to create a threat, along with serviceable torpedoes, which made the U-boat come of age. In this respect, the development of reliable internal combustion engines by 1918 was more influential than most individual weapons.

These technologies became effective during the war, partly because of the need to find solutions, but also because of the ability to integrate them into a wider arsenal of military hardware. Each individual design was not a war-winner in its own right, but deployed in conjunction with other weapons, could prove irresistible. The first use of flamethrowers and gas (February and April 1915 respectively), and tanks in September 1916 all proved disappointing, chiefly because

▲ German soldiers deploy flamethrowers in a throwback to the Ancient Greeks

they were used on their own. The one surprising area where technology failed to advance in 1914-18 was in communications, whose primitive nature failed to give commanders a real-time sense of battle, and held back the conduct of campaigns.

23 THE DEVELOPMENT OF DOCTRINE

As the BEF grew larger and mortars, large numbers of machine-guns, poison gas, flamethrowers, hand grenades, tanks and aircraft arrived on the battlefield, it became vital to coordinate these new technologies into its operations in a measured, formal way.

Technological change ensures that military doctrine needs to stay current, and the arrival of tanks in 1916 illustrates this. Many of the earliest tank attacks failed because infantry-armour-artillery tactics were not co-ordinated. This was because none had been rehearsed beforehand, because no doctrine was written. Once corrected and tactics devised and taught, the 1917 near-victory at Cambrai suggested what could be achieved with careful thought and preparation.

For the British, the first day of the Somme was the result of teaching very basic doctrine to large numbers of citizen volunteers. It was afterwards realised while that tactics needed to be more complex, the troops needed to understand them.

Thus, the BEF did not 'stand still' in doctrinal terms, as is often thought, but learned and fine-tuned their approach to battle every day. All soon understood that in the absence of real-time communications, doctrine was one of the few ways that senior commanders could influence a battle and overcome the 'fog of war'.

Doctrine cannot remove the confusion, but can help simplify decision-making. It also insures that all the elements of an army will view similar situations in similar ways. One of the problems on the Somme was that every attacking division assaulted in a different way, producing mixed results – there was no common approach. This was particularly important in a war with large armies of men who were not professional troops, but temporary soldiers with a limited knowledge of fieldcraft.

The BEF's ultimate triumphs of late 1918 were the results of much thought and learning, with army-wide doctrine taught to all participants beforehand. However, at the tactical level, the BEF's doctrine had to tread a fine line between setting rules and encouraging judgment and personal initiative.

◄ Lack of co-ordination resulted in costly lessons to be learnt, such as early tank deployment

ALAMY X2, PRESS ASSOCIATION

The British grand fleet on her way to meet the German fleet at the Battle of Jutland

24 THE BATTLE OF JUTLAND

Jutland (or Skagerrak to the Germans) was the biggest naval battle of the Great War, a clash of 151 British to 99 German warships. Both sides wanted the encounter: Vizeadmiral Reinhard Scheer wished to ambush part of Britain's Grand Fleet, denting its superiority, whilst Admiral Sir John Jellicoe hoped to destroy the German High Seas Fleet, once and for all. Jellicoe needed to be cautious however, for, as Churchill warned, he "could lose the war in an afternoon".

Indicating the shape of things to come, the Germans were spotted by a Short 184 seaplane from HMS *Engadine*, the first carrier ever to see action. On 31 May 1916, the German battlecruiser force (40 ships) under Vizeadmiral Franz von Hipper engaged Vice Admiral Sir David Beatty's cruisers (52 ships) about 75 miles from the Danish coast at 1548hrs, and was joined 55 minutes later by the rest of Scheer's fleet. Beatty (whose men included the future George VI on HMS *Collingwood*)

quickly lost three major ships, but he managed to fight his way towards the British Grand Fleet, speeding south to join him. When Scheer realised he had now encountered the entire British fleet, he sought to extricate himself and, despite a second fleet-to-fleet encounter, aided by a combination of British signalling blunders, cautious tactics and luck, managed to escape under cover of darkness.

The result was disappointing for the British, who lost 14 warships – three battlecruisers, three cruisers, eight destroyers and 6,094 dead. The Germans lost 10 vessels – one battleship, one battlecruiser, three cruisers, five destroyers and 2,551 killed. Although Jutland saw Germany inflict greater damage upon the Royal Navy, the Kaiser forbade a repeat performance, leading to a strategic victory for the British. Germany thereafter relied on its submarine fleet to bring the naval war to its opponents.

25 THE HORROR OF THE SOMME

Haig's intention was to mount a major assault with the French astride the River Somme, but he was forced to strike early, to distract German attention from Verdun. His plan was simple: Fourth Army was to punch through the German trenches, followed by the Reserve (later renamed the Fifth) Army, who would roll up the remaining defences. A diversionary attack would be launched in the north.

The battleground was a series of chalk ridges, into which the Germans had tunnelled extensive fortifications. A massive artillery bombardment to destroy the defences started on 24 June and lasted a week, with 1.7 million shells fired (of which up to 30 per cent failed to explode). Despite this weight of firepower, many German gun positions or barbed-wire defences remained intact, a fact not realised when the assault was launched.

On 1 July, infantry in waves followed a protective artillery barrage, but most were caught and killed on the intact wire. The losses were staggering – 57,470 officers and men, of whom 19,240 were killed, 2,152 missing, the rest wounded. However, in the south, witnessed by Siegfried Sassoon, the German front line was breached in places and ground gained.

Twelve battles constitute the July–November campaign; the 38th (Welsh) Division suffered taking Mametz Wood; Delville Wood fell after six days, where the South Africans lost heavily. On 15 September, tanks made their first appearance at Flers-Courcellette. It ended on 18 November, when the 51st Highland Division took Beaumont Hamel.

By November, the Germans were exhausted, pulled back and regarded the Somme as a defeat. The overall British casualties for the 142 days of fighting were some 415,000 men, but the Germans are calculated to have suffered much more – possibly 650,000. The French contributed 11 divisions, often overlooked – along with the 200,000 casualties they sustained – but in terms of manpower, resources and casualties, the Somme remains a British and Commonwealth battle.

▶▶▶ THE SOMME – PAGE 56

▲ The Battle of the Somme produced devastating casualties for all sides over 142 days of fierce fighting

US LIBRARY OF CONGRESS, GETTY, ALAMY

27 THE LIMITATIONS OF THE ITALIANS

Italy joined the Allied side in April 1915, declaring war on the Central Powers in May. This was ill-timed opportunism, in the hope of territorial expansion, as the Italian Army was poorly equipped and under-trained. Its commander, Luigi Cadorna, was uninspiring, had a poor grasp of leadership and was highly unpopular from his introduction of decimation (literally the execution of every 10th man) for under-performing units.

The Italians were backward logistically, with an inadequate medical service, poor roads and an inability to move men, guns and supplies efficiently through the Alpine terrain of northern Italy. In the end, uniforms, guns and equipment had to be given by France, Britain and the USA in order for Italy to sustain her operations. Ernest Hemingway, an ambulance driver on this front, captured the atmosphere of the theatre in his 1929 novel *A Farewell To Arms*.

Cadorna initiated 12 attritional battles along the river Isonzo over 1915-17, which gained nothing, and was caught off balance by the Caporetto campaign of 24 October 1917. Preceded by storm troops (including Erwin Rommel's unit), an Austro-German force pushed the Italians 70 miles back to the Piave river, prompting Britain and France to rush troops to Italy, fearing a collapse. A year later the Italo-Franco-British forces attacked at Vittorio Veneto on 24 October 1918 and had so overwhelmed the Austrians within five days that an armistice was requested and signed on 3 November.

Benito Mussolini was typical of many Italians at first, welcoming the conflict. He joined the army and rose to the rank of corporal, but was wounded by a mortar bomb in February 1917. He went on to edit a newspaper with a pro-war stance, but grew bitter when Italy gained very little at the Treaty of Versailles afterwards. By then, the war, with its casualties and rationing, had become unpopular with much of the nation. It cost Italy some 600,000 killed and 950,000 wounded, of whom 250,000 were crippled for life.

▲ South Africans hold a memorial service at Delville Wood, the site of severe losses against the Germans

26 THE SOUTH AFRICAN MASSACRE AT DELVILLE WOOD

All the British Empire forces were severely bloodied during the Great War, and the Union of South Africa's turn came on the Somme, with the capture of Delville Wood outside the village of Longueval from 14 July-3 September 1916.

Brigadier-General Henry Lukin's all-volunteer 1st South African Brigade, comprising 3,155 officers and men, was part of the 9th Scottish Division, which assaulted Longueval and Delville Wood beyond on the morning of 14 July. Tenacious German defence of Longueval absorbed two of the division's brigades, and the reserve (the South Africans) was ordered to 'take the wood at all costs' the following day.

Although the four battalions of South Africans twice attempted to clear the wood, the defenders were too strong; thereafter they survived vicious German counter attacks and continuous shelling between 15-20 July, and their battle in Delville became a tale of grit and endurance. One of their number, Private William Frederick Faulds, was awarded a Victoria Cross for his bravery, and soldiers in neighbouring units won a further three, indicating the ferocity of the engagements.

Hand-to-hand fighting amongst the oaks, hornbeams and beech trees caused many casualties, but German artillery inflicted more, it being impossible to dig in due to tree roots. When relief troops finally arrived in the South Africans' positions on the afternoon of 20 July, just three wounded officers and 140 men were able to march out. Their successors found Delville Wood just as difficult and the Germans were forced out only on 3 September.

The 63-hectare wood was acquired after the war by South Africa and a memorial to the 229,000 officers and men who served, and those 10,000 who died, was opened in 1926. Today, it houses a fine museum about South Africa's contribution to the First World War.

▲ Luigi Cadorna was unpopular, especially following his introduction of decimation – the execution of every 10th man – for under-performing units

28 THE BATTLE OF PASSCHENDAELE

The medieval town of Ypres lies at the centre of a bowl, with higher ground to the north, east and south, though the difference in height is barely evident. Continuous shelling from German guns on the surrounding heights almost levelled it. From Ypres in 1917, the Allies set out to punch through the strongly-defended Hindenburg Line, assault the Passchendaele Ridge and eventually reach the Belgian coast.

Passchendaele thus became shorthand for the Allied Third Ypres campaign, begun on 31 July 1917 and fought over four miles of terrain between Ypres and the Passchendaele Ridge, on which stands a small town of the same name – and, today, the Tyne Cot

Commonwealth War Cemetery, the largest Commonwealth war cemetery in the world. The ridge represents the furthest extent of the Allied advance, reached on 10 November 1917 after 103 days of heavy fighting.

Third Ypres opened following the successful seizing of the Messines Ridge between 7-14 June 1917. Prolonged shelling over the previous three years had obliterated the field drainage system in the low-lying salient, and coupled with abnormally heavy rain, the battlefield soon became a swamp. The area became synonymous with the misery of trench warfare, and Haig's decision to prolong rather than suspend the attack in such

▲ Australian troops pick their way through the devastation at Chateau Wood

conditions raises justifiable criticism of his generalship.

Soldiers were soon aware of the irony of fighting in an area called Passchendaele – the Valley of the Passion. So many Commonwealth and German soldiers were killed on this gently rising ground that we do not have an accurate count of the war dead: best estimates hover around 325,000 Allied and 260,000 German soldiers, killed, wounded and missing.

'Wipers' (the soldiers' name for Ypres) is most often associated with the futility of the First World War, prompted perhaps by Siegfried Sassoon's famous line, 'I died in hell - they called it Passchendaele', penned in November 1918.

29 CANADA'S ATTACK ON VIMY RIDGE

This five-mile long whale-back ridge of chalk in north-east France was the focus of continuous fighting throughout 1914-17. North of Arras, it rises to a height of 200 feet and overlooks the Lens coalfields, offering strategic advantages to whoever possessed it. The Germans captured Vimy in 1914, and the French suffered 150,000 casualties trying to win it back in 1915. Vimy became a British sector in February 1916, and both sides tunnelled extensively, exploding underground mines, digging trenches and shelters. The ridge also concealed German gun positions and observation posts.

In 1917, it was the target of an attack by Julian Byng's Canadian Corps, comprising nearly 100,000 Canadians in four divisions – the first time Canadians fought as a single formation on the Western Front. Their success rested on a fire plan, partly devised by Major Alan Brooke (the future Chief of the Imperial General Staff of the Second World War), which included a thousand guns targeting every German artillery piece.

New flash-spotting and sound-ranging techniques, using observers, optics and microphones, identified all German positions. To preserve surprise, tunnels were dug to move troops to the front lines, as well as large underground chambers where soldiers could wait before battle.

Launched in blinding snow at 5.30am on 9 April 1917, it surprised the Germans. The artillery programme was a great success, protecting the infantry and destroying many German guns. All four Canadian divisions broke through the lines, and within a day had captured the high point of Hill 145. By 12 April, the 4th Canadian Division had seized their last objective, The Pimple, and Vimy was secure.

▲ The Vimy Ridge Canadian War Memorial contains areas of preserved trenches

---

30 RESPECTFUL BURIALS

From August 1914, although armies recognised the importance of the prompt and reverent burial of the dead, the sheer volume of slaughter overwhelmed them. The nature of the fighting immediately produced thousands of soldiers whose bodies were either obliterated by technology or recovered too mutilated to identify.

Initially, the British kept few records of burials but, from September 1914, encouraged by Fabian Ware (1869-1949), director of a Red Cross unit, they developed an organisation for registering and maintaining graves. Ware's unit grew and through his vision was retitled the Graves Registration Commission in March 1915. It became the Imperial (from 1960, Commonwealth) War Graves Commission, by Act of Parliament on 21 May 1917. Responsible also for graves away from the Western Front, it soon acquired the responsibility for maintaining all cemeteries and memorials, as well as recording the slain. Ware's organisation now tends 1.75 million war dead worldwide and inspired both the American Battle Monuments Commission and the German Volksbund Deutsche Kriegsgraberfursorge.

The CWGC generally avoided mass burial sites (which can become political statements), and although there are huge concentration cemeteries like Tyne Cot outside Ypres, at 12,000 graves the largest anywhere, most are much smaller. The Somme battlefields contain 280 graveyards and the Ypres area 160, some with just a handful of burials. Allies and enemies rest alongside Commonwealth servicemen, regardless of rank or creed.

Whilst the Menin Gate Memorial in Ypres, recording 54,389 of the 'missing', and the Thiepval Memorial on the Somme battlefields, with 72,194 inscribed names, have become the focus of renewed interest and commemoration, the CWGC cemeteries and memorials were always designed to be powerful statements of national culture, reflecting the unity of the fallen, the Christian concept of sacrifice and hope of resurrection. The best architects of the day designed them, with their well-tended flowers and shrubs and Portland Stone, to resemble English gardens.

◀ Sir Fabian Ware's War Graves Commission continues to oversee Commonwealth war graves to this day

31 LEADERSHIP TRAINING

British officer statistics were staggering. Of the 247,061 who held a King's Commission during 1914-1918, four per cent were captured, 30 per cent wounded, and 13.5 per cent were killed, totalling 116,781 – or to put it another way, nearly one in two. Where were such numbers of officers found?

Regulars became officers after 18 months at Sandhurst (for the infantry and cavalry) or two years at Woolwich (engineers and gunners). Cadets were required to pay for their education – at £100 a year – as well as uniforms and other equipment, but had to pass competitive examinations for entry. No leadership was taught to officers, as most were privately educated, trained at school to lead and serve their country or Empire. The war caused Sandhurst to be shortened to three months, Woolwich to four.

The Territorials also continued to commission officers through the war, most having the same background and education as their regular counterparts. Territorial officers were taught basic military skills, but not leadership, and the main criteria for selection was attendance at a Junior Officer Training Corps (OTC, run in most public schools) or a Senior OTC (on each university campus). OTCs commissioned some 20,577 officers in 1914-15 and eventually 100,000.

When the Kitchener volunteers formed into battalions from August 1914, there was a huge need for officers, and none to spare. Some battalions, because of the high quality of their middle-class recruits, gradually became officer commissioning units – including the Artists Rifles, who would produce over 10,000 officers – but there was no co-ordination, and it was left to the whim of commanding officers as to who was commissioned.

In February 1916, Officer Cadet Battalions were established, where candidates of any background or rank were taught, not assumed to be, leaders. Considered very successful, this method

▲ The Artists Rifles, seen here with Douglas Haig at St Omer, provided over 10,000 officers

replaced casualties and kept pace with army expansion, granting over 73,000 temporary commissions to 116,781 officer candidates. By 1918, well over half of the 164,255 officers would have been promoted through the ranks.

32 THE ARRIVAL OF TANK WARFARE

Cambrai Day – 20 November – is celebrated by Britain's Royal Tank Regiment as the first occasion when tanks were used in appropriate numbers or with specially devised tactics of their own. After an uncertain debut on the Somme in 1916, and use over appalling terrain at Passchendaele, belief in the tank as a war-winner had waned. Yet commanders had been agitating for an operation where they could demonstrate what tanks were

capable of achieving. Used en masse, they argued, tanks could be a powerful psychological weapon against defenders and a decisive one for attackers.

For Cambrai, almost 500 (mostly the improved Mk IV) were concentrated and crews trained in new tactics, which required accompanying infantry to overcome enemy artillery – the 77mm field gun being the tanks' main opponent. As expected, the tanks overwhelmed

the German first line on 20 November 1917 and had achieved all their initial objectives by midday. Unfortunately at Flesquières, the 51st (Highland) Division ignored the new doctrine, hung back and allowed German gunners to pick off the armour, shattering the mystique of tanks as indestructible.

After the first day, 180 tanks were out of action and the defenders were able to plug holes with reinforcements. Tanks had broken in, but failed to break through. Rushing in masses of fresh troops by road and rail, the Germans counter-attacked on 29 November, regaining much of their lost ground, and the usual stalemate followed

The lack of British reserves was crucial to the outcome, but Passchendaele had absorbed all spare troops, and Cambrai is now seen as a lost opportunity. Casualties were, unusually for a Great War battle, both low and even at 45,000 for the British and Germans. In November 1998, one of the original tanks, D51 'Deborah', was discovered on the old battlefield at Flesquières, where it had lain buried for 80 years.

◄ Tank D51 'Deborah' was recovered from the battlefield in 1998 and is today housed in a private barn in Flesquières

PRESS ASSOCIATION, TOPFOTO, WESTERNFRONTPHOTOGRAPHY.COM /

33 RUSSIA'S REVOLUTIONS

Russian military performance was lamentable – unimpressive gains made for crippling casualties, while the Imperial court in Petrograd (formerly St Petersburg) seemed impervious to the horror.

In an attempt to strengthen his own reputation, Tsar Nicholas departed to take personal charge of his army, thereafter linking the crown with an unpopular war. Domestic power was left in the hands of his wife. Formerly Alexandra of Hesse – a German – the Tsarina was considered suspect and under the thumb of Rasputin.

Factories were incapable of making good equipment, while shortages of raw materials led to a slump in output, prompting mass unemployment. In February 1917, discontent spilled over into strikes and demonstrations; streets filled with white-collar professionals and factory workers.

When Nicholas ordered his army to quell the riots by force, troops mutinied and officers were shot or went into hiding. Symbols of the Tsarist regime were torn down and governmental authority collapsed. Nicholas was advised to abdicate, which he did on 15 March, being placed under house arrest with his family by Alexander Kerensky's provisional government.

Although Russia had already suffered huge losses, Kerensky continued with the war, depressing morale and triggering thousands of desertions every month. While Bolshevik agitators fuelled discontent, Kerensky's policies of removing officers' authority and giving sweeping powers to soldiers' committees only worsened the situation, and his administration became discredited. Brusilov's July offensive then failed with high casualties, which proved the final straw. The army disintegrated and revolution spread.

On 25 October, Lenin's Military Revolutionary Committee began to seize official buildings and the Winter Palace in Petrograd, which led, inevitably, to Russia leaving the war.

Among the revolutionaries was Josip Broz Tito, a Croat serving in the Austrian army. Captured in 1915, he joined Lenin's Reds in 1917. Following Brest-Litovsk, among the many German prisoners returning home were those indoctrinated with Communism. They would soon throw themselves into the post-war revolution that undermined Germany.

▼ Workers in Petrograd march demanding an eight-hour day

34 THE SALONIKA CAMPAIGN

In early 1915, Britain and France discussed opening a Balkan campaign as a way of realigning military strategy after the onset of stalemate on the Western Front. The various policy options were hotly debated between 'easterners' and 'westerners'. The former saw it as a way to persuade neighbouring states to throw in their lot with the Allies and force an end to the deadlock in France. The latter (including most British generals) considered it a distraction. When a campaign based on the Greek port of Salonika (today, Thessaloniki) finally got underway in October 1915, it arrived too late to assist Serbia – the original justification – but continued as a base for operations against pro-German Bulgaria.

As the months passed, the allied commitment to the Salonika campaign steadily increased with the addition of the reconstituted Serbian Army as well as Italian, Romanian and, after the Allies had deposed King Constantine in June 1917, Greek forces. At its peak the allied army numbered some 600,000 men.

By contrast, the Germans progressively withdrew from the campaign. In March 1916, Falkenhayn abandoned plans for a large-scale offensive in the Balkans in order to concentrate on the attack at Verdun. This left a largely Bulgarian force of about 450,000 men tying down the numerically stronger Allies. The grateful Germans thus came to look upon Salonika as the largest internment camp of the war.

Militarily, the campaign was largely irrelevant to the outcome of the war until the last few weeks of fighting. Then, in mid-September 1918, an advance under the new allied commander, Franchet d'Espérey, produced a rapid disintegration in the Bulgarian forces, which the German commander Ludendorff later concluded had been a decisive factor in his country's defeat. High in the hills overlooking the port the front line trenches still remain, now covered by scrub.

▲ British soldiers use periscopes in a Salonika fire trench, August 1918

▲ T. E. Lawrence became a symbol of First World War heroism

35 THE ROMANCE OF LAWRENCE OF ARABIA

Lionised by Peter O'Toole in the 1962 film *Lawrence of Arabia*, Thomas Edward Lawrence was a brilliant history student at Oxford, who went on to study in Syria and Mesopotamia, while assisting a British military survey of the area.

During the war he was attached to Military Intelligence in Egypt and, in October 1916, appointed liaison officer to the tribes in revolt against Turkish rule. Befriending their leader, Faisal, he organised and led a series of guerrilla attacks on railways throughout the region, the route by which Turkish reinforcements arrived. He became Faisal's political and military advisor, acquired British money and military support for the revolt and, in July 1917, they captured the Red Sea port of Aqaba.

Lawrence might have remained an obscure, eccentric warrior, but for his 'discovery' by the American journalist Lowell Thomas. Lawrence, in his flowing white robes, riding a camel to war, provided exactly the romantic figure American readers wanted, rather than tales from the 'stale' Western Front. Lawrence's profile coincided with the arrival of Allenby in Palestine and, with the latter's support, he captured Damascus in October 1918. After declining the rewards of a colonelcy, CB, DSO and French Croix de Guerre, Lawrence (in his robes) sparked interest at the Paris and Cairo Peace Conferences, where he promoted Arab independence and unity.

His account of the desert revolt, *Seven Pillars of Wisdom*, was published to world acclaim two months after his death. In 1985, a group of British soldiers retraced some of the actions and journeys he described. Riding camels, they discovered that some of his claims and exploits were open to challenge and concluded that, whilst not a charlatan, Lawrence had exaggerated and embellished his own role in the revolt. Nonetheless, this engaging man clearly possessed personal charisma and was a born guerilla leader.

36 WAR IN EAST AFRICA

This often-overlooked campaign was a series of battles and guerrilla actions that started in German East Africa (today's Burundi, Rwanda, and Tanzania) and spread over Mozambique, Northern Rhodesia, British East Africa, Uganda and the Belgian Congo.

The strategy of the German colonial forces, led by Lieutenant Colonel Paul von Lettow-Vorbeck, using his tiny force of 260 Germans of all ranks – formerly colonial administrators – and 2,500 locally recruited Askaris, was to distract vastly superior Allied forces away from the Western Front. In this he was remarkably successful, and carried on fighting until the armistice, tying down troops and formally surrendering only on 25 November 1918.

His techniques included a series of raids and ambushes on British bases and settlements producing commodities vital to the war effort, but he rarely stayed to fight, always melting away before superior numbers. In one of the few pitched battles at Mahiwa in 1917, the Germans lost 500 killed and wounded but the opposing British Nigerian brigade lost 2,700.

His successes brought von Lettow-Vorbeck some reinforcements, but his force never exceeded 1,800 Germans and some 12,000 Askaris. By contrast, the British and Empire forces totalled nearly one million men in their fruitless pursuit of Lettow-Vorbeck (who was later promoted to Generalmajor in recognition of his achievements) and his handful of warriors. His successful strategy made him a role model for many later guerrilla leaders.

British forces, who operated in independent marching columns, comprised regular battalions of King's African Rifles and Indian army troops, Rhodesians and South Africans, including Boers and British. Because of the vast logistics involved, nearly 400,000 Allied soldiers, sailors and administrators participated in the East Africa campaign, supported in the field by 600,000 African porters.

The British and Empire forces lost over 10,000 men, and many more African porters, the majority from disease. Thousands also died in the influenza epidemic that swept the world in 1918-19. German losses were about 2,000.

▲ Tanzania, as part of German East Africa, saw remarkable German successes despite being vastly outnumbered by the British

▶▶▶ *Turn to page 86 for the closing instalment of* The Story of the War *to discover how the course of the war changed dramatically in its closing months*

British reserve troops wait to move up to the front line at the Somme. More than 127,000 of them would never return from these particular killing fields

THE SOMME

GETTY

A TERRIBLE LEARNING CURVE

Nearly a century on from the infamous First World War battle
where many thousands of soldiers died, **Gary Sheffield** explains
what British generals learned from the bloodbath

Soldiers from the Border Regiment take rest during a quieter moment of the drawn-out battle

CORBIS, IMPERIAL WAR MUSEUM, MARY EVANS PICTURE LIBRARY, TOPFOTO

Today, the northern part of the Somme battlefield is dominated by the huge Memorial To The Missing at Thiepval in northern France. Here are inscribed the names of 72,085 soldiers of the British Expeditionary Force (BEF) who were killed but who have no known grave.

Before the First World War, there was a chateau and a village here, but in the summer of 1916 it became the site of a bitter battle that lasted for nearly three months. The memorial offers mute testimony to the disastrous first day of the Somme, a day that has become synonymous with military incompetence.

Yet a short distance away, on the site of the chateau, is another memorial – an obelisk on a plinth. This commemorates 18th (Eastern) Division, which finally captured Thiepval on 26-27 September 1916. It was an operation that demonstrated how much the BEF had learned from the fighting on the Somme.

The army that was committed to battle in July 1916 was composed largely of green wartime volunteers, enthusiastic but poorly trained. The pre-war experience of the army and its commanders in colonial small wars – even a relatively large conflict like the South African War (1899-1902) – was not good preparation for the Western Front. Fighting a

The British army had too few heavy guns to achieve its task of destroying enemy positions

high-intensity conflict against a first-class enemy like the German army made huge demands on soldiers of all ranks – and 1915 was a painful year of trial and error. The situation was exacerbated by the fact that the British army was simultaneously expanding, while the conduct of war was undergoing changes so profound that historians have subsequently labelled it a "revolution in military affairs".

Two years later things were very different. In the 'Hundred Days' that began with the Battle of Amiens of 8 August 1918, described by the German commander Ludendorff as the "black day of the German Army", the BEF took the lead in winning a decisive military victory.

Complex picture
Historians have debated the extent, nature and speed of the BEF's learning curve. In reality, there was not one learning curve, but several. For instance, arguably, the change in infantry tactics on the Somme outpaced the absorption and application of lessons by senior commanders. Moreover, some military units were more effective at identifying and internalising lessons than others and, once recognised, lessons were not always applied consistently. For all that, there is compelling evidence that the learning curve of the BEF was real, if uneven.

What happened at Thiepval on 1 July 1916 was all too typical of that terrible

◀ Sir Ivor Maxse, one of the best trainers in the British army

day. A formation of Kitchener's army volunteers, 32nd Division, was given the formidable task of capturing the Thiepval Spur, one of the toughest positions on the Somme front. German engineers had methodically converted a village of about 100 houses into strongpoints. Close by was the Leipzig Redoubt, a defensive work from which machine guns could fire into No Man's Land. There were further redoubts to the flanks and the rear of the German positions. Both armies recognised the Thiepval Plateau for what it was – dominating ground that had to be taken if the British attack was to make progress.

At 7.30am, the attack began. The men of 32nd Division's 96th Brigade clambered out of their trenches and were raked by perhaps 30 machine guns from Thiepval village. It was a massacre. Three battalions of volunteers from the north of England –1st and 2nd Salford Pals, and the Tyneside Commercials – could make little headway, although isolated parties got into Thiepval village. Worse was to come: reports that the village had actually fallen to 32nd Division led to the Royal Artillery ceasing to fire on this target.

Small victories

The attack by the 97th Brigade on the Leipzig Redoubt fared rather better. Brigadier-General JB Jardine, drawing on his experience of observation of the fighting in the Russo-Japanese War 11 years before, ordered his men to get out of their trenches while the British artillery were still pounding the German positions. The Glasgow Commercials crept to within 30 or 40 yards of the German front line. When the barrage lifted, the infantry were able to race forward and get into the German trench before the defenders could properly respond.

Leipzig Redoubt was taken and held, but the weight of fire was such that 32nd Division could not get any further forward. The fact that, within the same division, one brigade used effective tactics while another did not is a good indication of the hit-and-miss nature of the British army's learning process in mid-1916.

On 1 July 1916, the British army had too few heavy guns for the job that it was given – that ▷▷

▲ German prisoners carry a wounded British soldier during the assault on Trônes Wood

The names of more than 72,000 British soldiers killed without proper burial adorn the memorial in Thiepval

THE SOMME IN CONTEXT

How, despite phenomenally large Allied losses, the war's most notorious battle was more damaging to the Germans

The Battle of the Somme was fought from 1 July to 18 November 1916 on the banks of the eponymous river, between the French towns of Albert (on the Allied side of the lines) and Bapaume (on the German side). The battle stemmed from the failure of the belligerents to reach a compromise peace, despite the military stalemate on the Western Front. This was largely because the Germans would not relinquish the territory they had captured in France and Belgium, while the French would not contemplate a peace without German troops first being expelled from their national territory.

At the end of 1915, it was decided that the British and French would launch a major offensive on the Western Front in the following summer, in combination with attacks on other fronts by their Russian and Italian allies. In the event, the German attack at Verdun in February 1916 forced the French to commit forces to defend this key sector, and it was the British army, rather than the more experienced French, that made the biggest contribution to the battle. Hopes of a major breakthrough on the Somme faded after the failure of most of the initial British attacks, and it became an attritional battle in which both sides suffered enormous casualties in struggles for places like Pozières, Thiepval and High Wood.

On balance, the Somme did more damage to the Germans than to the Allies, and in spite of the heavy losses, the British army emerged from the battle as a much improved effective fighting force.

▲ A bloodstained tunic worn by Second Lieutenant Harold Cope, wounded during an attack on Delville Wood, 7 August 1916

KEY POINTS ON THE LEARNING CURVE

The British army learned some definite – if painful – tactical lessons from the bloodbath on the Somme.
These lessons were to transform its ability to wage war, and helped bring about Germany's defeat in 1918

British troops of the Seaforth Highlanders at a roll call after the first day of the Battle of the Somme

1 1 July 1916 ▲

The British attack begins, but in most places makes little headway. British artillery fails to cut barbed wire, or suppress German guns, machine guns and infantry. The tactics of many infantry units are clumsy and the success on the southern flank is not exploited.

2 14 July 1916 ▶

Bazentin Ridge is captured at dawn. Surprise is achieved by the infantry assembling at night and the artillery bombardment lasting for only five minutes. High Wood seems to be there for the taking, but problems in bringing forward the cavalry delays exploitation of this success and the Germans are able to rush up troops to restore the stalemate.

◀ A wallet and pocket book belonging to Robert Smylie, who died on 14 July 1916, with a letter from a friend expressing his grief

GETTY X2; IMPERIAL WAR MUSEUM X2; MARY EVANS PICTURE LIBRARY X3

A British Mark I tank, C.19 'Clan Leslie', in Chimpanzee Valley on 15 September 1916, the day tanks first went into action

The sky is lit up by the bombardment of enemy lines prior to the assault of Thiepval

3 15 September 1916 ▲

The Battle of Flers-Courcelette. Some ground is gained but the Allies fail to achieve a breakthrough. In some places, effective tactics are used, with the tank making its debut. The artillery is still given too much to do and the front of the attack is too wide. Clearly, some lessons have been learned; some haven't.

4 26 September 1916 ▲

The capture of Thiepval by 18th Division. Maxse's men benefit from careful preparation, rigorous training, a limited and achievable objective, up-to-date tactics and effective use of artillery. The day before, similar advantages help the Fourth Army achieve a striking success at Morval a few miles south.

5 13 November 1916 ▶

The Battle of the Ancre. Beaumont Hamel, an objective on 1 July, is captured by 51st (Highland) Division. The Highlanders are aided by an effective creeping artillery barrage, the support of tanks, and concentrated machine gun fire. Their assault is well planned, and starts only 250 yards from the German trenches.

6 9 April 1917 ▼

The first day of the Battle of Arras. This is the day that the experiences of the Somme really begin to pay off. Trained in the new tactics codified over the winter months, the successes at the beginning of this battle demonstrate the extent to which the lessons of the Somme have been absorbed and applied.

The flooded Ancre Valley, one of the crucibles of fighting during the latter stages of the Battle of the Somme

British troops march into position in April 1917 at Arras, where they enjoyed early success

British soldiers with a captured German machine gun during the Battle of Amiens

7 8 August 1918 ▲

The Battle of Amiens. The lessons learned on the Somme and Passchendaele come to fruition as the British army's weapons system comes of age. Combined with an effective operational plan, the Allies inflict a devastating defeat on the Germans and follow it up with a series of heavy blows that only end with the German capitulation on 11 November 1918.

▶

STATISTICS OF THE SOMME

The scale and logistics of one of the First World War's bloodiest battles makes for a dizzying numbers game – for both sides

127,751
British soldiers who died during the Battle of the Somme, July to November 1916

893
average number per day of British soldiers who died during the Battle of the Somme, July to November 1916

419,654
British casualties during the Battle of the Somme, July to November 1916

204,253
French casualties during the Battle of the Somme, July to November 1916

465,000–680,000
estimates of German casualties during the Battle of the Somme, July to November 1916

100,000
number of horses required by British army for first stage of Somme offensive

74,000
number of rounds of ammunition fired by German defenders of Serre on 1 July 1916

7
number of miles advanced by British during the Battle of the Somme, July to November 1916

1,000,000
number of rounds of ammunition fired by British 100th Machine Gun Company on 24 August 1916

42
German divisions diverted to the Somme in July and August 1916

▷▷ of destroying the enemy positions. What's more, the available guns were given too many targets to bombard, catastrophically reducing the concentration of firepower. Moreover, infantry tactics were often crude.

Practice and preparation

But even in the midst of disaster there were signs of hope, of some units employing methods that worked. One of the formations on the right of the British line was 18th Division. Its commander, Major-General Ivor Maxse, had a reputation as one of the best trainers in the British army. Indeed, before the battle, his men had thoroughly rehearsed their assault.

The artillery fired a creeping barrage, by which a curtain of shells moved steadily ahead of the infantry, and this helped 18th Division take all its objectives. Two weeks later, it captured Trônes Wood and, in September, Maxse's men attacked Thiepval. In a hard three-day action, this German bastion finally fell to the British.

In his after-action report, Maxse stated that "with sufficient time to prepare an assault on a definite and limited objective, I believe that a well trained division can capture almost any 'impregnable'

stronghold, and this doctrine has been taught to the 18th Division".

Maxse brought in a senior staff officer to lecture on "recent fighting experiences on this front" and the tank was incorporated into the battle plan. Maxse limited the objectives to be captured, and attacked at 12.35pm, rather than in the morning, so as to minimise the hours in which his men, having captured the German trenches, could be shelled in daylight.

An officer of 18th Division wrote that "everyone was full of confidence. The troops were trained to the minute; attack formations had been practised until it could be expected that the advance would push through to its final objective as a drill movement, whatever the obstacles or casualties. It was known, too, that the artillery preparation had been terrific." In short, Thiepval was an excellent example of the learning curve in action, but it was far from the only one.

Lessons learned

The Germans also learned lessons from the Somme and other battles. They moved away from defending linear trenches to a much looser and more flexible system of defending strongpoints and using reserves in the counter-attack role.

They abandoned their policy of automatically counter-attacking every Allied gain. But, ultimately, they learned a wrong lesson. By concentrating resources on a relatively small number of elite 'storm' units, they reduced the overall quality of their army. In the long run, this proved to be a disastrous policy.

By April 1917, when it fought its next major battle, the BEF was a far more effective force than nine months earlier

Over the winter of 1916-17, the lessons of the Somme were collected and analysed by the British, and formed the basis of two important tactical manuals issued in February 1917. Three months later, when it fought its next major battle in April, the BEF was a vastly more effective force than it had been nine months earlier.

On the first day at Arras, British divisions advanced more than three miles, while Canadian and British troops seized the vital ground of Vimy Ridge. There was a long way to go, but the BEF continued to learn

▶ The imposing Thiepval Memorial to the Missing of the Somme which pays tribute to more than 72,000 missing soldiers

and apply the hard-won lessons of battles such as Passchendaele. By the summer of 1918, it had reached a peak of efficiency.

It is not going too far to say that the lessons of the Somme laid the foundations for the extraordinary series of victories of the Hundred Days that brought the war to a successful conclusion. ⊞

Gary Sheffield is Professor of War Studies at the University of Birmingham and the author of several books on the First World War, including *The Somme* (Cassell, 2004)

Watch an animated map of the Battle of the Somme on the BBC website
➜ bbc.in/QdGqww

▼ British troops of the Liverpool Rifles walk towards the German lines during the attack on Ginchy, September 1916

SOLDIER SPORTSMEN

Many sporting stars enlisted and lost their lives during the First World War. **Clive Harris** and **Julian Whippy** recall the exploits of these inspiring men, revealing poignant tales of their bravery and heroism

As the Edwardian era heralded the mass spectator interest in sport for recreational purposes, footballers, rugby players, tennis stars and cricketers became household names. Some were worshipped by their public and courted by the media, while others were uncomfortable in the public glare and continued to apply a Corinthian spirit to their sport.

On the declaration of war, the authorities agreed that this was no time for games, but they also realised the recruiting potential such games brought at sporting venues across Britain.

Around the globe men flocked to join the colours alongside their idols. Edgar Mobbs, the English rugby star, was key in filling the ranks of the 7th Northamptonshire Regiment, a unit he would command before his death at Ypres in July 1917.

Arthur Jones, an Australian rules footballer from Fitzroy in Melbourne, joined the Light Horse mounted infantry unit along with fellow players and supporters, only to be killed at Gallipoli in August 1915. Many enlisted in the 'sporting battalions' of Kitchener's new army, notably the 17th Middlesex and 16th Royal Scots for footballers, while the 11th King's Royal Rifle Corps raised a platoon of professional golfers who even brought their caddies. ⊞

Clive Harris and Julian Whippy are military historians and co-authors of *The Greater Game: Sporting Icons Who Fell In The War* (Pen and Sword, May 2008)

FURTHER READING

▶ *When The Whistle Blows: The Story Of The Footballers' Battalion In The Great War* by Andrew Riddoch and John Kemp (Haynes Publishing, 2011)

FOOTBALL
ALEX 'SANDY' TURNBULL

Turnbull played for both Manchester teams *Above:* His FA Cup-winning goal for United

■ The first draft of men received in France by the 8th East Surreys after their successful but costly advance on the Somme was addressed by the quarter master: "This is a sporting battalion, and they make good fighting battalions. If any of you have any sporting prowess make yourself known to me!"

The battalion that had famously kicked footballs into the attack a week earlier led by Captain Wilfred 'Billy' Neville were surprised to find among the new ranks Alex 'Sandy' Turnbull. Turnbull had won the FA Cup with Manchester City in 1904 before crossing the city to United in 1905. There he went on to score the winning goal in the 1909 Cup Final.

While serving at the front, he both led the 8th East Surreys to victory in the divisional cup and was promoted to Lance Sergeant for gallantry. Loved by his men, he sadly met his death at Chérisy in north-east France on 3 May 1917 during the Battle of Arras. Along with Walter Tull, the pioneering black Spurs player who was commissioned during the war, Turnbull is commemorated on the Arras memorial to the missing.

CORBIS X2, DREAMSTIME X2, GETTY X3

Wilding drove armoured Rolls Royces in the war

TENNIS
TONY WILDING

■ With ten Grand Slams to his credit, including seven Wimbledon titles, New Zealander Tony Wilding also won the Davis Cup four times and earned a bronze medal in the 1912 Stockholm Olympics. He played cricket for Barbados and entered motorcycle races across Europe en route to tennis tournaments. Engaged to Broadway actress and society pin-up Maxine Elliot, his exploits filled the tabloids of the day.

In 1914, he joined the new Armoured Car Section as a Royal Marine officer in the Royal Naval Air Service. Racing around the roads of Belgium, with a relaxed attitude to discipline, this band in their Rolls Royce cars with boiler plate armour and machine guns became known as 'The Motor Bandits'.

Wilding commanded a dismounted gun crew for over 12 hours in the Battle of Auber's Ridge until killed by a shell on 9 May 1915. Identified only by his gold cigarette case, he never smoked but carried them for gentlemen who did. He is buried in the Rue-des-Berceaux Military cemetery in France.

CRICKET
COLIN BLYTHE

■ Colin Blythe, the England and Kent left-handed slow bowler, took more than 2,500 wickets in his first-class career from 1899 to 1914. He came into top-flight cricket by fluke. While standing at the nets on Blackheath before a Kent-Somerset match in 1897, he was invited to "bowl a few" to the Kent all-rounder Walter Wright. His talent was obvious and he was selected for the Kent academy.

Poor health affected his army fitness classification and he first spent time garrisoned in Kent. By 1917, pressures on the supply of fit young men led to him being drafted to the 12th King's Own Yorkshire Light Infantry.

This unit was charged with building trenches and laying railways at Ypres. On the night of 8 November, a random shrapnel shell exploded over the heads of Blythe's working party. A shard of jagged metal pierced his tunic, slicing through the photograph of his wife Jane. Blythe was fatally wounded and buried nearby. It is believed that an Edwardian cricket ball, supposedly left by a battlefield pilgrim, lay at the foot of Blythe's nearby grave right up until the 1980s.

Kent and England bowler Colin Blythe died in 1917

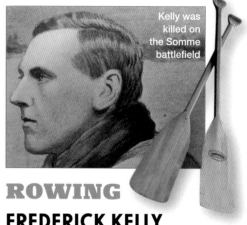
Kelly was killed on the Somme battlefield

ROWING
FREDERICK KELLY

■ In 1908, one of the first ever rowing gold medals for Britain hung around the neck of Frederick Septimus Kelly, an Olympian who served in the Royal Naval Division.

Australian-born, he was sent by his wealthy trading father to Eton to complete his education. Having become a member of the Leander Rowing Club of Henley he excelled in the coxed eights and rowed in the University Boat Race.

As a well-connected member of high-society London, the list of those advising Kelly on which army corps to join reads like a who's who of the Great War. Lord Kitchener, Winston Churchill and Prime Minister Herbert Asquith all offered guidance.

Having joined the Royal Naval Division, Kelly served at Gallipoli, where he was awarded the Distinguished Service Cross. As acting lieutenant commander in Hood Battalion, he was to die in the Battle of the Ancre, on the Somme battlefield. The Division was attacking Beaucourt-sur-Ancre when Kelly was seen trying to knock out a machine gun post. He was fatally wounded in the process.

ICE HOCKEY
FRANK 'ONE EYE' McGEE

■ Among the Commonwealth sporting icons who fought and fell was Canada's Frank McGee. As the star of the Ottawa Senators, a side that dominated ice hockey in Canada between 1903 and 1906, he once famously scored 14 goals in a single Stanley Cup game against the Dawson City Nuggets. His heroics also included an injury-time winner against the Rat Portage Thistles to maintain the title. The winning goal led to wild scenes on the streets of Canada.

His career was all the more incredible given the loss of sight in one eye during a Boer War fundraising game. In 1914, he was commissioned into the 21st Central Ontario Battalion of the Canadian Expeditionary Force and wounded at Hill 62 in 1916 while operating an armoured car. After a spell recuperating in a training role, he rejoined his battalion for the Battle of the Somme. He was killed at Courcelette on 16 September 1916, fending off a counter-attack at the head of his men.

Frank McGee, pictured with his Ottawa Senators team-mates in 1905

1914

Sunday

Haig shakes hands with
officers of the Second
Canadian Division in
December 1918

A MAN MUCH MISUNDERSTOOD?

Field Marshal Haig has gone down in history as the general who callously sent hundreds of thousands of Tommies to their deaths – one of the 'donkeys who led the lions'. But, through their analysis of Haig's diaries, **Gary Sheffield** and **John Bourne** have arrived at a rather different view of the war leader

Field Marshal Sir Douglas Haig has had the unenviable reputation of being the worst British general of all time, a bone-headed "donkey" who threw away the lives of his men in futile attacks. In many ways, the debate has now moved on from such stereotypes. Certainly, a revolution in the historiography of the First World War has occurred over recent years.

Most historians now agree that by 1918 the British Army had become a highly skilled, technologically advanced force that played a leading role in defeating the Germans. However, Haig's role is still a matter of dispute. Was he, as the late John Terraine claimed, a "great captain"? Or was Haig, as Tim Travers has argued, a relatively marginal figure in the eventual Allied success? Or does the truth lie somewhere in between?

For years, the lack of a modern scholarly edition of Haig's voluminous writings hampered a proper reassessment of his command. The publication of *Douglas Haig: War Diaries and Letters* in 2005 gave the opportunity to assess Haig afresh.

An important item on the charge sheet, made by Denis Winter in his Haig's Command in 1991, is that Haig falsified his diaries in an attempt to cover up his incompetence. Now, it is certainly true that there are two versions of the diary, one handwritten at the time, one typed by Lady Haig after the war, and there are some differences between them.

Most are trivial – Haig added details or improved his grammar – but some are significant. The only

> **There are two versions of the diary, one handwritten at the time, one typed by Lady Haig after the war. And there are differences between them**

previous edition, edited by Robert Blake in 1952, was flawed in that it was based on the typed diary, and did not differentiate between the two versions. The 2005 edition was based on the original manuscript, with major differences indicated in

square brackets, a practice we have followed here. Haig used the typed version to provide more details or to gloss the text with his opinions, as in the entry of 3 April 1918:

Before the meeting broke up, I asked the Governments to state their desire that a French offensive should be started as soon as possible in order to attract the enemy's Reserves and so prevent him from continuing his pressure against the British. Foch and Pétain both stated their determination to start attacking as soon as possible. [But will they ever attack? I doubt whether the French Army as a whole is now fit for an offensive.]

In several instances, diary entries from the two sources are very different, but even here, as Elizabeth Greenhalgh has argued, the changes expand, rather than contradict, the original. The overall authenticity of Haig's diary is, however, not in doubt. The fact that Haig did not destroy the original manuscript diary undermines the notion of a sinister conspiracy.

In considering the picture of Haig that emerges from his ▷

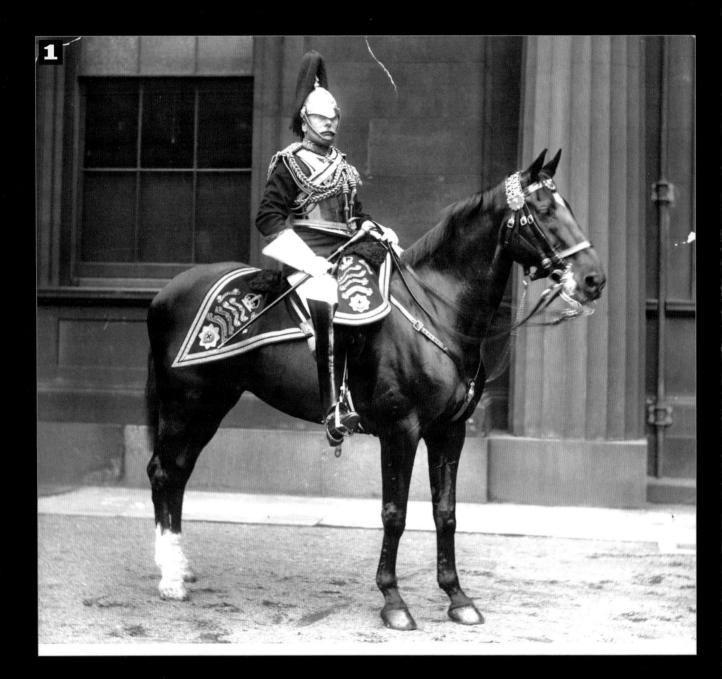

'Total casualties [on the first day of the Somme] are estimated at over 40,000 ... This cannot be considered severe in view of the numbers engaged' (2 July 1916)

1. **A very Victorian soldier?** Haig had a reputation as a technophobe – unfairly, since he was an enthusiastic supporter of air power, tanks and modern artillery

2. **Allies in France** (left to right) French General Joffre, French President Poincare, King George V, French General Foch (supreme commander of the Allies) and Haig, c 1916

3. **Another Napoleon?** Haig and Foch inspect troops. Haig wrote that Foch, who became supreme Allied commander in 1918, had a 'swelled head'

4. **Edinburgh boy** Douglas Haig (1861-1928), shown here around 1870, was born into the Scottish whisky distilling family

5. **A good marriage** Haig received great support from his wife, the Hon Dorothy Vivian (above right). They married in 1905 and had four children

▷ papers, we have to bear in mind that he, and his army, were products of a very different society from today's. Thus attitudes towards authority, patriotism and the toleration of casualties are poles apart from the modern mind-set. Britain was fighting a war of national survival and Haig should be judged by the standards of his time, not by those of the 21st century.

As commander of the largest army that Britain has ever put in the field, Douglas Haig had a huge burden of responsibility. The circumstances of the Western Front, where even successful battles produced horrific casualties, can only have increased the pressure. He coped with the strain of high command in a number of ways. One was to impose some psychological distance. A good example is found in his diary entry for 2 July 1916, the day after the notorious "First Day on the Somme":

A day of downs and ups! … The A[djutant] G[eneral] reported today that the total casualties are estimated at over 40,000 to date. This cannot be considered severe in view of the numbers engaged, and the length of front attacked …

To a modern eye, this appears appallingly callous. However, it is important to note Haig faced, on a vast scale, the dilemma of all generals in history: their decisions inevitably lead to the death and wounding of their men. To cope with this awesome responsibility, generals have to develop a "mask of command": the gift of self-control, especially the ability to appear calm in a time of crisis. Haig's apparent callousness was in fact part of the mental make-up possessed by every successful commander. Generals who dwell on the reality of sending men to their deaths crack up.

In reality, Haig felt deeply for the men under his command. As a Victorian army officer, he was imbued with a profound sense of paternalistic responsibility for his soldiers. While he was not a man who wore his heart on his sleeve, his inner feelings sometimes broke through. In January 1915, he wrote to his brother about the terrible conditions endured by "the poor d---ls in the trenches". An entry such as that for 18 September 1914 also hints at Haig's concerns:

I visited some of the wounded. The Ambulance personnel have been much overworked. Dressings are very short. Horse ambulance wagons no use; light motors (like what the French have) most necessary.

The paternal ethos of Haig and the British officer corps was responsible for the creation of a vast ▷

▷ organisation dedicated to the welfare of the soldier. This was in part a pragmatic way to maintain military morale, but it also reflected a long-standing tradition that with the privileges of the officer came responsibility for his men.

It is obvious from reading his papers that two things in particular sustained Haig: his family and his religion. In 1905, Haig married the Hon Dorothy (Doris) Vivian, maid of honour to Queen Alexandra, after a whirlwind courtship. It has been implied that Haig married purely to curry royal favour, or even that he sought to distance himself from homosexual patrons. The evidence of the diary and of Haig's letters to his wife show clearly that the marriage was a real one. Doris's constant love and support was of vital importance to him during the war. They had four children, on whom Haig doted. This diary entry for 26 November 1914 during a period on leave is typical:

I walked to the War Office with Doris. I Saw General Sclater (Adjutant General) and discussed the class of man sent out as drafts … At 1 o'clock we lunched at Princes Gate with the children, and spent a happy afternoon at the Zoo. The Houses were locked up before we came away, so that they did not see the monkey house, a disappointment … but they saw

▼ Haig wrote that the first day's estimated 40,000 casualties at the Somme "cannot be considered severe".

every other kind of animal very well and fed them.

We can see that Haig spends part of one of his precious days at home working, but in order to maximise their time together Lady Haig walks with him (and patiently waits outside for the meeting to end). Then he enjoys quality time with his young family.

Another charge levelled against Haig is that he saw himself as

> **'Latest Drafts are young, but men have been well trained … One officer said they are "like the young Soldiers at Waterloo, and will again save the Empire"'** (8 May 1918)

God's chosen instrument, that this sense of destiny fuelled a selfish ambition, and made him careless of casualties. Under his mother's influence, he developed the habit of prayer, a sense of "divine oversight" and an easy familiarity with scripture. The diary is littered with entries like the one for 11 November 1917:

I attended Church of Scotland at 9.30am. Reverend Captain Duncan officiated. Text from 90th Psalm Oh Lord Thou hast been our dwelling place for all generations. A most encouraging sermon at this time.

There is no doubt that Haig drew great strength from his Christian faith, and Duncan's sermons in particular. Many other senior army officers were also devout. However, Padre Duncan was not a firebrand Old Testament preacher, but rather a sophisticated liberal academic

theologian, and Duncan himself categorically denied that Haig was a "religious fanatic".

Much has been made of Haig's pre-war dabbling in the realms of spiritualism. However, we have discovered no new evidence on this particular subject, and thus can safely be dismissed as a major influence on the Field Marshal during the First World War.

Haig's popular reputation stands or falls on his performance as a battlefield commander, but in fact his role was far wider. A typical diary entry (18 January 1918) reads: "Colonel Bacon … arrived as head of the American Mission and I had a long talk with him".

Bacon would have been one of hundreds, if not thousands of visitors Haig met during the war. Haig was in overall control of British military operations on the Western Front, but was also senior British commander in the Allied coalition and theatre commander, responsible for administration and liaising with the government. Today, two or even three individuals would share these responsibilities. Arguably, Haig simply had too much to do.

Much of his time was spent dealing with allies. Haig frequently paints the French in a less than flattering light. On 27 October 1918, he noted that the French

…are doing their utmost to get control of everything! Consequently, there is much friction in the Balkans and in Palestine and in the fleet in the Mediterranean! It is odd that the French should be so greedy of power! … It seems that Clemenceau and Foch are not on good terms. Foch is suffering from a swelled head, and thinks himself another Napoleon!

However, like many diarists, Haig used his journal to vent his frustration, and his actions with regard to the French belie his words. He was essentially a loyal and co-operative ally, who recognised that co-operation was essential if victory was to be achieved. In 1918, Haig formed a spiky but productive partnership with Foch, the supreme commander, while Haig's drive and vision were of vital importance in the critical last 100 days of the war.

Haig's mature attitude to his allies was an indication of the breadth of his vision, but was far from being the only one. In August 1914, he was one of the few British decision-makers who saw that the war was unlikely to be over by Christmas:

I held that we must organise our resources for a war of several years … Great Britain must at once take in hand the creation of an Army. I mentioned one million as the number to aim at immediately.

Although Haig has the reputation of a technophobe, the truth is very different. He was an enthusiastic supporter of air power, tanks, artillery and machine guns. His enthusiasm can be seen in a diary entry for 12 December 1914:

I inspected some trench mortars [which we are making in our

Engineer workshops. They are made of steel piping,] about 2 feet long, with a movable support near the muzzle to alter the elevation … They fire a bomb of 2lb weight.

As the war drew to an end, the Allies began to think of the terms on which they were prepared to make peace with Germany. From mid-October 1918, Haig began to be more pessimistic about the possibility of inflicting a decisive defeat. Accordingly, he advocated that the Germans should be offered moderate peace terms. In retrospect, he grossly under-estimated the scale of the Allied victories and their effect on the Germans, but he was influenced by intelligence assessments that proved to be erroneous, or out of date.

In reality, Germany, and its army, was collapsing. Haig was painfully aware that British strength and influence would decline – and that of the United States increase – the longer that the war dragged on. He also feared the spread of Bolshevism, should existing authority collapse. He reasoned that a lenient peace might avert the prospect of both prolonged fighting and Communist revolution. In the event, the 1919 Versailles Treaty, settled by politicians not soldiers, achieved the worst of all worlds – too harsh for the Germans to be easily conciliated, without taking away their ability to recover and make war.

▲ On his death in 1928, Haig was popularly seen as a national hero. But within just 10 years, his reputation had been greatly eroded

Douglas Haig, like any other general, made mistakes – and the circumstances of the Western Front meant that his mistakes produced an appalling number of casualties. But he also presided over an army that emerged as a technologically advanced and enormously effective force that won the greatest series of victories in British military history, against a background of changes in warfare so great they amounted to a revolution in military affairs. ⬢

Gary Sheffield is Professor of War Studies at the University of Birmingham. Now retired, **John Bourne** was the director of the Centre for First World War Studies, also at the University of Birmingham

Read more from Gary Sheffield on the Lions vs Donkeys debate on the BBC website ➲ **bbc.in/OPook3**

'Certainly some of the Tanks have done marvels! and have enabled our attack to progress at a surprisingly fast pace' (15 September 1916)

DID CONKERS HELP WIN THE FIRST WORLD WAR?

Saul David explains how Britain's schoolchildren were enlisted into the war effort – via the humble horse chestnut, the staple of the playground game of conkers

I n the autumn of 1917, a notice appeared on the walls of classrooms and scout huts across Britain: "Groups of scholars and boy scouts are being organised to collect conkers… This collection is invaluable war work and is very urgent. Please encourage it."

It was never explained to the children exactly how conkers – otherwise known as horse chestnuts, the essential tool of the popular playground game – could help the war effort. Nor did they care. They were more interested in the War Office's bounty of 7s 6d (37.5p) for every hundredweight they handed in. For weeks they scoured woods and lanes for the shiny brown objects they usually destroyed in the game.

The children's efforts were so successful that there simply weren't enough trains to transport them. Piles were seen rotting at railway stations. But a total of 3,000 tonnes of conkers did reach their destination – the Synthetic Products Company at King's Lynn – where they were used to make acetone, a vital component of the smokeless propellant for shells and bullets known as cordite.

Cordite had been used by the British military since 1889, when it first replaced black gunpowder. It consisted chiefly of the high-explosives nitroglycerine and nitrocellulose (gun-cotton), with acetone playing the key role of solvent in the manufacturing process. Prior to the First World War, the acetone used in British munitions was made almost entirely from the dry distillation (pyrolysis) of wood. As it required almost a hundred tonnes of birch, beech or maple

▲ Boys playing conkers in 1919. Horse chestnuts played an unlikely role in the war effort just a few years earlier

▶ Chaim Weizmann, the chemist who came up with the idea of harvesting conkers for highly prized acetone

▲ The cordite factory in Dorset, where the Admiralty converted grain to acetone

▼ A female munitions worker straightens out strings of cordite ready for packing

to produce a tonne of acetone, the great timber-growing countries were the biggest producers of this vital commodity, with Britain forced to import the vast majority of its acetone from the United States.

An attempt to produce its own acetone was made in 1913 when a modern factory was built in the Forest of Dean in Gloucestershire. But by the outbreak of war in 1914, the stocks for military use totalled just 3,200 tonnes and it was soon obvious that an alternative domestic supply would be needed. This became even more pressing during the spring of 1915 when an acute shortage of shells – the so-called 'shell crisis' – reduced some British guns to firing just four times a day.

Alternative methods

The British government created a dedicated Ministry of Munitions, run by the future Prime Minister David Lloyd George. One of Lloyd George's first initiatives was to ask the brilliant chemist Chaim Weizmann of Manchester University if there was an alternative way of making acetone in large quantities.

There was. Developing the work of Louis Pasteur and others, Weizmann had perfected an anaerobic fermentation process that used a highly vigorous bacterium known as *Clostridium acetobutylicum* (also known as the Weizmann organism) to produce large quantities of acetone from a variety of starchy foodstuffs such as grain, maize and rice. He at once agreed to place his process at the disposal of the government.

In May 1915, after Weizmann had demonstrated to the Admiralty that he could convert 100 tonnes of grain to

12 tonnes of acetone, the government commandeered brewing and distillery equipment, and built dedicated factories to utilise the new process in Dorset and Norfolk. Together they produced more than 90,000 gallons of acetone a year, enough to feed the war's seemingly insatiable demand for cordite. (The

There weren't enough trains to transport all the conkers the children gathered

British army and Royal Navy, alone, fired 248 million shells from 1914 to 1918.)

But by 1917, as grain and potatoes were needed to feed the British population, and German U-boat activity in the Atlantic was threatening to cut off the import of maize from the United States, Weizmann was tasked to find another supply of starch for his process that would not interfere with the already limited food supplies. He began experimenting with conkers, aware that they grew in abundance across the country, and found that the yield of acetone was sufficiently high to begin production. This, in turn, prompted the nationwide appeal for schoolchildren to collect the conkers and hand them in.

The government was determined not to reveal the real reason for the great chestnut hunt of 1917 in case the blockaded Germans copied their methods. The only official statement was printed in *The Times* on 26 July 1917.

It read: "Chestnut seeds, not the green husks, are required by the Government for the Ministry of Munitions. The nuts

will replace cereals which have been necessary for the production of an article of great importance in the prosecution of the War."

When questions were asked in the House of Commons, the veiled response was that the conkers were needed for "certain purposes". So suspicious did some members of the public become that they accused the government of using voluntary labour for private profit.

The actual production of acetone from conkers was, despite Weizmann's assurances, never that successful. Teething problems meant the manufacturing process did not begin in the Norfolk factory until April 1918, and it was soon discovered that horse chestnuts did not provide the yields the government had hoped for. Production ended after just three months.

So did conkers really help to win the war? They played their part, certainly, even if their role was more walk-on than centre stage. The real star of the show was Chaim Weizmann, whose brilliant solution to the acetone shortage – using a variety of natural products from maize to conkers – helped to solve the shell crisis and get Britain's guns firing again. **H**

Saul David has presented numerous history programmes on the BBC network

The first American soldiers land in France, wearing their 'sombrero' pre-war campaign hats

"A war against all nations"

The United States might not have joined the fighting until 1917 but, as **Doran L Cart** explains, it became fully committed to the Allied war effort

"Vive les Teddies" the French people yelled while they threw roses at American soldiers, who stuffed the flowers into their campaign hats and rifle barrels. This scene in Paris on 3 July 1917 was one of the early acts in the play of the American land forces' involvement in the First World War.

The 'Teddies' – or 'Sammies', 'Yanks' or the soon-to-be ubiquitous 'Doughboys' – were indeed now part of an incredible undertaking on the global stage. As an anonymous American volunteer serving with the French Army related early on, "they are the new world, they wear the uniform badly but their teeth are a brilliant lesson of beauty and health to the *poilu*

[French infantryman]. They are charming and mysterious and unaccountable."

President Woodrow Wilson called on Congress to declare war on Germany on 2 April 1917. The official declaration came four days later. The country had tried to stay out of the war, but by that spring, international conditions, including Germany's unrestricted submarine warfare strategy, forced the United States' hand.

The debate on whether or not to enter the war was one of the most contentious in American history. Many German-Americans saw the war simply as one to save the British Empire. Irish-Americans, a key constituency for President Woodrow Wilson, opposed alliance with Britain,

Ireland's oppressor. People in the western and southern states accused East Coast businesses of promoting the war, while socialists and radical labour unionists felt that American workers should keep out of Europe's capitalist struggles.

Before 1917, the US had never participated in European politics, nor had it ever fought a major war outside North America. Many Americans believed their country had no reason to fight in this conflict. President Wilson had just won re-election with the slogan 'He Kept Us Out Of War', while the year's hit song was *I Didn't Raise My Boy To Be A Soldier*.

In the early months of 1917, however, German policies became more provocative. Sensational headlines reported each new development, raising apprehensions about what future course the country would take. Americans began to realise that they might not be able to avoid the conflict after all.

Change of opinion

On 1 March, the American public learned about a German proposal to ally with Mexico against the US. Months earlier, British intelligence intercepted a secret message from Arthur Zimmermann, the German Foreign Secretary, to the Mexican government. It was an invitation for Mexico to join Germany and Japan in a war against the US. The lure was that Mexico would recover the south-western states it had lost in the Mexican War of 1846-47.

On 2 April, Wilson went before a special session of Congress to request a declaration of war. Germany's new submarine policy, he charged, "is a war against mankind. It is a war against all nations." He also spoke about German spying inside the US and the treachery

of the Zimmermann telegram. The German government, he said, was a "natural foe of liberty" and that "the world must be made safe for democracy".

The US was completely unprepared to fight in a global war but, by late June 1917, the first soldiers arrived in France. They were the vanguard of the American Expeditionary Forces (AEF). The US Navy had been involved in convoy duty in the Atlantic for some time – by 1 December 1917, parts of four divisions had arrived in France.

The Americans, from every walk of life, came to the colours by volunteering or through conscription. Each had his or her own story. For many, it was a chance to work at tasks unavailable to them in the regular circumstances of society. For others, especially for African-Americans, the war for liberty did not apply to their situations at home.

It became an adventure, a chance to see the world, even though it was a world at war. Many couldn't wait for April 1917 and they volunteered to serve the Allies in many capacities.

Their presence was felt in a number of ways, often in sheer numbers. For instance, one single division in the American Expeditionary Forces was huge in comparison to those of other armies; by 1918, it numbered 27,082 men. The Americans were quick into battle, too. The first combat troops of the 1st Division occupied a front-line position near Nancy on 21 October 1917, with the first artillery round fired at the enemy two days later.

Sectors, towns, rivers and woods soon became part of the American military history lexicon: the Marne Salient, the Aisne Defensive, Belleau Wood, ▷

◀ The US 6th Field Artillery Regiment 75mm gun crew on duty in the Ansauville Sector

▷ Montdidier-Noyon Defensive, Aisne-Marne Offensive, Champagne-Marne Defensive, Audenarde and the Vosges.

The 5th Marines had all landed in France by 3 July 1917 and were originally part of the 1st US Army Division. Later combined in September with the 6th Marine Regiment and the 6th Machine Gun battalion, the 5th Regiment was assigned to the 2nd Division, US Army.

The Marines' grim experiences were documented by Dean Robertson of the

The American forces came well-equipped, with the US Navy boasting the war's heaviest mobile guns. Mounted on railroad cars, they had a range of 45,000 yards

79th Company, 6th Regiment. He wrote that "we are in the fields – not in the trenches. You must have read what the Americans are doing and of the open fighting. Everyone is a fatalist here. It is hard to dodge a shell and when your time comes it's going to get you. The Marines are sure doing their part and I am proud to belong."

The Americans proved themselves very efficient in battle. A telegram sent at 9:30am from the 1st Division on 28 May 1918 quickly summed up the momentous action of that morning:

"The Twenty Eighth infantry attacked Cantigny six forty five AM. All objectives gained seven thirty AM. Feeble German reaction up to present moment. One hundred forty five prisoners including two officers counted no information

regarding our losses. We successfully attacked and took Cantigny. It is impossible to estimate the enemy's losses in killed and wounded, but they are very heavy. Our casualties are estimated to be about 300."

The reality of war
American forces came well-equipped. In the fall of 1918, the US Navy had the five heaviest mobile guns in action on the Western Front. Mounted on railroad gun cars, these 14-inch Mark I naval guns were manned by navy personnel, mostly wearing army uniforms. The guns' maximum range was 45,000 yards.

The ferocity of warfare certainly opened American eyes. Sergeant Charles S Stevenson, from the 314th Engineers, 89th Division, wrote on 18 September 1918: "This is the seventh day of the St. Mihiel drive and I find myself sitting in a thick, muddy forest, with my knees and a gas mask as a table, writing to you. It was *some* drive. Small, in comparison to many operations, to we rookies it was a *real* battle. Machine guns, rifles, shells, aeroplanes and tanks – everything you read about – I saw 'em all.

"We followed the first line (the attacking party) for 12 hours and ours was a sort of 'after the battle' review. I saw all kinds of German trenches, barbed wire entanglements, busted houses, burning trees, deep shell holes, torn-up railroad tracks, peaceful gardens, dynamited bridges. All kinds of German prisoners passed me on the way back."

Corporal John Lewis Barkley, of 4th Infantry Regiment, 3rd Division, was similarly enlightened by the nature of the fighting. He wrote: "How would you like to have been in the battle of the Argonne? ...There was a barrage from both sides of

▲ Female telephone operators from the US Signal Corps, three miles from the front line

▲ US Corporal John Lewis Barkley, recipient of the much-vaunted Medal of Honor

▲ American troops are patched up at a first-aid dressing station in September 1918

AMERICA
IN THE GREAT WAR

··· 7 May 1915 ···
The Cunard passenger liner *Lusitania* is sunk by German submarine U-20 in British waters. 1,198 people drown, including 124 US citizens.

··· 7 Nov 1916 ···
Democrat Woodrow Wilson is re-elected as US President on the slogan 'He Kept Us Out Of War'. The Republican candidate, Charles Evans Hughes, is perceived as a war-monger.

··· 31 January 1917 ···
Germans resume unrestricted U-boat campaign. Kaiser Wilhelm II orders "To all U-Boats – sink on sight".

··· 1 March 1917 ···
The US population is alerted about the Zimmermann telegram, which reveals a German plot against the US.

··· 2 April 1917 ···
Wilson delivers his war message to Congress, saying that the world must be made "safe for democracy". War is declared four days later.

25 June 1917
The first American troops land in France. General John J Pershing greets the infantrymen and engineers as they step ashore.

··· 28 May 1918 ···
The US 1st Division mounts an assault on the German observation strongpoint at Cantigny and, within 35 minutes, secures the village.

··· 6 June 1918 ···
At Belleau Wood, US Marines launch an attack against the German position on the banks of the Aisne River.

··· 12-16 September 1918 ···
Commanded by George Patton, the fledgling 304th Tank Brigade draws its first blood at St Mihiel.

··· 26 September – 11 November 1918 ···
US Meuse-Argonne Offensive is the most important battle for the Americans in the war.

shrapnel and the strongest of gases and the biggest of guns. The Germans shot some of the damnedest shells at us you ever heard of – bigger than nail kegs and four times as long and when one hit you had better watch out." Barkley was later awarded the Medal of Honor, the highest American decoration, for bravery, for his actions in the Meuse Argonne battle.

American women served the American Expeditionary Forces in all duties except as combat soldiers, although some died as a direct result of artillery shelling. They were doctors and nurses. They drove heavy trucks and ambulances. They sang and entertained and translated. Signal Corps telephone operators worked near the front lines. One observer wrote that they "do anything they were given to do; that their hours are long; that their task is hard; that for them there is small hope of medals and citations and glittering homecoming parades."

Debatable contribution
The American contribution to the outcome of the fighting on the Western Front, the Italian Front and the war in general has been widely discussed, debated and written about. The Americans either tipped the scales for the Allies or they failed miserably. As in every army, a wide range of human frailties and strengths were shown. Incredible acts of individual and unit bravery took place next to cowardice and awful field leadership.

But, regardless of what the Americans did or did not do for the outcome of the war, global economic, political, territorial and military issues had been greatly affected by the American involvement in the war and the peace process.

The US commitment to the Allied effort was sizeable. More than four million Americans were in uniform, with one and a half million of those serving overseas. 50,385 were killed in action and 54,754 died of disease. A further 260,000 were either wounded or disabled in action.

The American efforts on the ground during the war were summarised by the American Expeditionary Forces Commander-in-Chief, General John J Pershing, on 12 November 1918 in his message to his troops:

"Our armies, hurriedly raised and hastily trained, met a veteran enemy, and by courage, discipline and skill defeated him. Without complaint you have endured incessant toil, privation and danger.

"You have seen many of your comrades make the supreme sacrifice that freedom may live. I thank you for the patience and courage with which you have endured. I congratulate you upon the splendid fruits of victory, which your heroism and the blood of our gallant dead are now presenting to our nation. Your deeds will live forever on the most glorious pages of America's history." ⬛

Doran L Cart has been the Senior Curator at the National World War I Museum in Kansas City, Missouri, for more than 22 years

NATIONAL WORLD WAR I MUSEUM / KANSAS CITY, MISSOURI / USA X3, THINKSTOCK

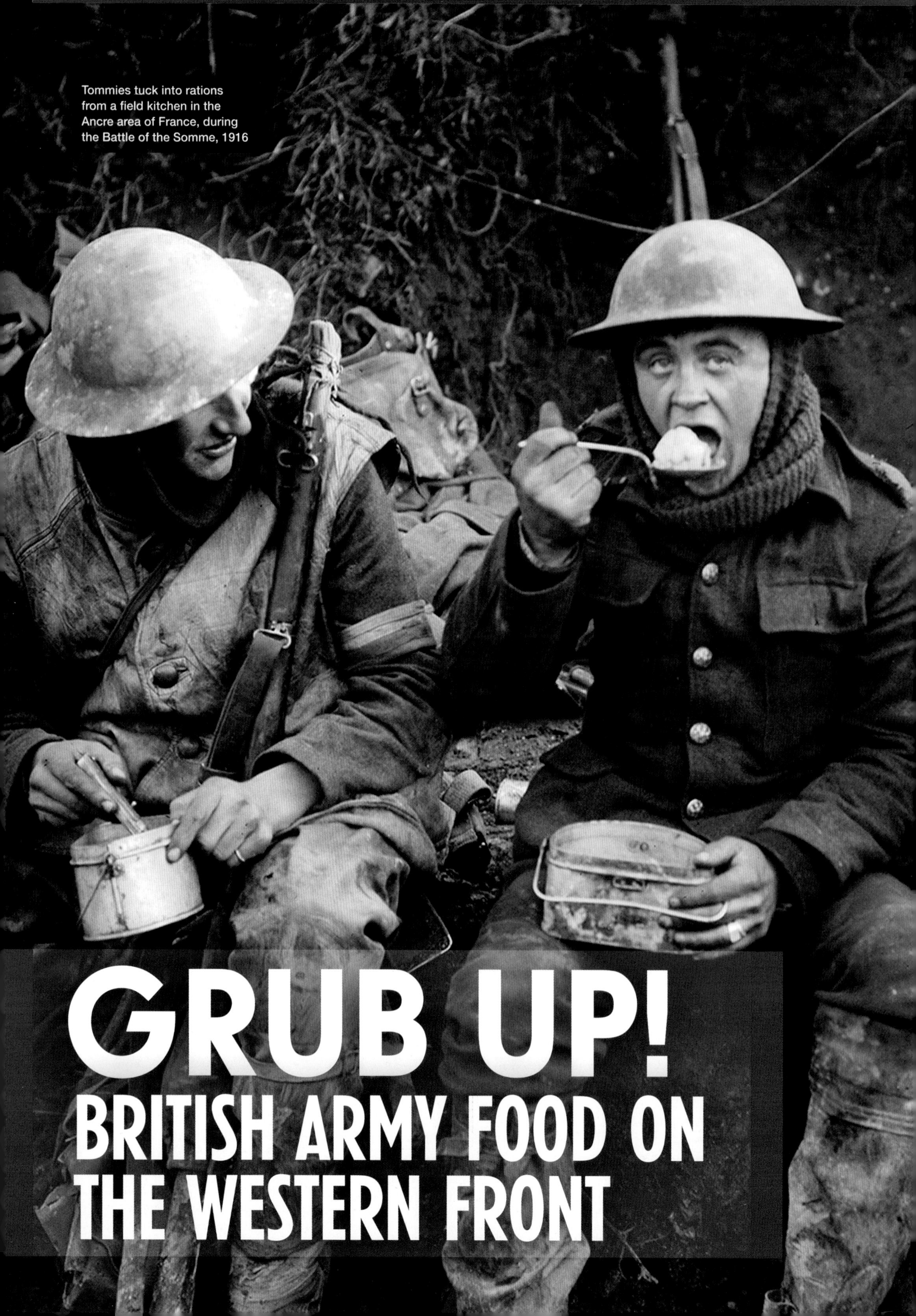

Tommies tuck into rations
from a field kitchen in the
Ancre area of France, during
the Battle of the Somme, 1916

GRUB UP!
BRITISH ARMY FOOD ON THE WESTERN FRONT

An army can't march on an empty stomach – but rations were far from haute cuisine. **Rachel Duffett** describes a diet based on rock-hard biscuits and bully beef

Private S T Eachus, a signaller with the Royal Engineers, kept a detailed diary of his wartime service in France and proved to be a stern critic of much he witnessed – from the strategy at the First Battle of the Somme to the excesses of army discipline. Yet he was at his angriest on 16 August 1916 when describing deficiencies in the food rations given to the troops: "Have heard a good deal about German atrocities, but certainly in some respect the British are quite as bad and cruel, for weeks together we have not had a second vegetable, often none at all."

Eachus wasn't joking. He had given up his liberty – and potentially his life – for his country and, at the very least, expected to be fed properly. His was a view widely shared by the rank-and-file soldiers of the war, whose letters, diaries and memoirs are replete with references to, and criticisms of, army food.

Perhaps unsurprisingly, the men's stories run counter to the official statistics and histories, which confidently proclaim the success of military feeding. On paper, the ration set for front-line rank-and-file soldiers does indeed appear generous at just over 4,000 calories per day, little different from today. As the war continued, reductions were made, mainly in the training and reserve camps, so preserving the best diet for those on active service. The daily scales for each soldier were highly detailed, from the key items of meat and bread (around a pound of each) through the three ounces of jam and two of cheese, to the half-ounce of salt and one thirty-sixth of pepper.

Field kitchens

Good cooks were able to convert the rations into tasty meals for the men. Private Sid Liddell wrote that the cooks were "really splendid. Besides the usual stews, roasts, plum duffs, etc, we have had stewed rabbit & pork, stewed mixed fruits & custard, rice pudding & fruit."

However, not all were as conscientious or able, despite the army training 92,627 new cooks during the conflict. Lance Corporal Walter Holyfield expressed a widely held view when he wrote to his mother that "our cooks are manuals; they'll turn a lump of the finest steak into a rough chip of mahogany in no time".

Formal complaints about the cooks were unwise. Someone at Private A E Perriman's camp complained to the regiment ▷

IMPERIAL WAR MUSEUM

▷ sergeant major that the tea was disgusting with "grease from the previous meal floating on top". The sergeant bellowed "there's nothing wrong with that", proceeding to stir the offending beverage with his fingers.

The soldiers' appetites would have been better satisfied if the specified rations had been delivered in full. Supply in war is fraught with difficulty and at times, such as during the chaotic retreat from Mons in 1914, provisioning broke down completely. Sergeant T H Cubbon recorded that, on 5 September 1914, he had not eaten for 36 hours. A week later, he complained that he'd only received half a tin of meat and two hardtack biscuits over a similar period.

The static nature of the Western Front generally facilitated the delivery of food to the men through a complex system of trains, motor vehicles, horse-drawn limbers and handcarts. Base Supply Depots (BSDs) were established on the French coast to store the quantities of food required to feed the huge numbers of soldiers. By March 1918, the ration strength had reached 1,828,098. One hangar at Le Havre held 80,000 tonnes in a building more than half a mile long and over 600 feet wide. Bakeries were established near the BSDs – at Boulogne, 15,875,667 pounds of bread were issued in one month alone.

1. Soldiers with their Christmas dinners. The British Army tried to make the day festive

2. A French postcard showing a British travelling bakery in 1914

3. Orderlies prepare sandwiches for the wounded at the battle of Arras, April 1917

4. A range of the long-life food sent to the British troops on the front line

Space in the supply lines was always at a premium, so compact, calorifically dense food with a long shelf-life suited the army best. Tinned bully beef was easier to store, transport and serve than fresh or frozen meat, while hardtack biscuit was preferable to bread.

Alternative uses

Feeding men in distant and often dangerous front lines was difficult and the High Command regarded bully and biscuit as a useful solution to the problem – perhaps because they rarely ate it at HQ. The men in the trenches were less keen. The rock-like biscuit meant that even men with good teeth found it a challenge. For the many men with bad teeth – a consequence of the poor pre-war diet and lack of dentistry – it could verge on the torturous. It was a standing joke that biscuit made better kindling than eating; occasionally they were used as a canvas by the more artistic or a mount for cigarette cards, pleasing decorations for the dug-out. Ingenuity made the biscuit edible and 'pozzy', where it was ground up and boiled with a tin of milk and some jam, was popular.

Cooking in the trenches was permitted, but depended upon proximity to the enemy. Private W A Quinton recalled heating pierced tins of meat and vegetables on an open fire. "Usually it tasted badly of smoke," he wrote, "but it was appetising enough to a hungry stomach."

Cookhouses were established in forward positions, as the army knew how important hot food was to the men's morale. Where kitchens were forced to remain distant, pan-packs were developed so that ration parties could carry stew to the front on their backs. Travelling kitchens were also used.

Captain Sidney Rogerson thought the stews he tasted in his capacity were pretty good "even if, as sometimes happened, a kipper or two had found their way among the meat, vegetables and biscuits…"

The soldiers were often less tolerant of eclectic mixtures. Private Eric Hiscock recalled a pal moaning "the f***ing stuff's mule, and I don't care who hears me". In fact, mule or horse meat did unofficially find its way into the ration, as many units ate the animal casualties of shelling rather than waste the meat.

> **"Mule and horse meat did find its way unofficially into the ration, as units ate the animal casualties of shelling"**

The official army recipe books aimed to give the cooks clear direction on the best food for the men in their care. The 1915 *Manual Of Military Cooking And Dietary Mobilization* contains a complete 100-day menu schedule. However, the desire for variety was tempered by the need to ensure that the cookhouses made the most economical use of ingredients – and following the menu plan meant that the leftovers from one day could be included in the next day's dishes.

A subsequent booklet entitled *Cooking In The Field* contained a number of new recipes. Of course, 'new' was not strictly accurate: the ingredients must have induced a sense of déjà vu. Bully beef was the chief constituent, whether in 'bread soup' (bully with bread and stock) or 'potted meat' (minced bully with pepper). Even the optimistically named 'Fish Paste' was four tins of sardines mixed with eight tins of bully beef.

Although it was rare for the supply chain to break down completely, failure to provide the variety promised in the published ration scales was commonplace. Contemporary nutritional science emphasised the importance of calories and lacked a full understanding of the role of vitamins and minerals. Consequently, the military believed that the sacrifice of a varied diet to the expedient but monotonous bully and biscuit was unproblematic.

Of course, whatever efforts the army expended in its provisioning, it was always unlikely that it would satisfy the men. The soldiers' accounts show us what psychologists are well aware of: that eating is about much more than mere calories. Food's physiological role is inextricably linked with its complex social and emotional associations. The anger that men directed towards army food, like that of Private Eachus quoted at the start, had broader origins than the mess hall menu.

In common with many of his peers, Eachus's dissatisfaction with his rations said more about his resentment at fighting a war that terrified him, far away from the comforts of home, than it did a shortage of vegetables. **H**

Rachel Duffett is the author of *The Stomach For Fighting: Food And The Soldiers Of The Great War* (Manchester University Press, 2012)

Britain's flying aces

Many of us have heard of Germany's famed Red Baron. But, as **Peter Hart** reveals, two of the greatest pilots fighting for aerial supremacy were part of Britain's Royal Flying Corps

Most people have heard of Manfred von Richthofen, the dreaded Red Baron, scourge of the skies in the Great War. But Britain had its own heroes – men now largely forgotten in our modern age, aces whose successes were marked by a trail of shattered German aircraft. The greatest of these were James McCudden and Edward Mannock.

The Royal Flying Corps had only been founded in 1912 and just 63 aircraft had crossed over to France when the First World War started in August 1914. In retrospect, it is amazing how quickly the RFC matured. The original function of aircraft had been one of reconnaissance – a pilot and an observer with his notebook. Once trench lines developed, aircraft became the only method of finding out what was going on behind the German front line. Soon, cameras were taken up in the aircraft and the humble notebook was abandoned in favour of glass-plate photographs that exposed the location of German gun batteries, machine gun posts and dugouts.

But photographs were only the start. Using a wireless, aircraft could provide the corrections to range artillery shells directly onto targets that were invisible from the ground. The implications were to be far-reaching, for no army could now allow enemy aircraft that freedom above their lines. By 1915, both sides had developed the first scout aircraft designed to shoot down reconnaissance aircraft. Thus began the battle for control of the skies.

The cult of the 'ace' – men who had shot down more than five enemy ▷

▶ James 'Jimmy' McCudden scored a prolific 57 victories in the air and was awarded the Victoria Cross. He was killed at the age of 23

THOSE MAGNIFICENT MEN The aces in the British pack

◀ EDWARD 'MICK' MANNOCK

Edward Mannock was born on 24 May 1887 into a working-class family. While contract-working in Turkey, he was interned on the outbreak of war in 1914 and later released due to ill health. On recovery, he was commissioned and joined the RFC in 1916. He served with the 40th, 74th and 85th Squadrons on the Western Front between 1917 and 1918. He was shot down and killed on 26 July 1918. He is credited with 73 victories.

JAMES McCUDDEN ▶

James McCudden was born on 28 March 1895 into a working-class army family. He joined the Royal Engineers as boy bugler in 1910, but transferred to the Royal Flying Corps as an engine fitter in 1913. He was commissioned in January 1917, serving with the 3rd, 29th and 56th Squadrons on the Western Front. He was killed in an accident on 9 July 1918 having already been awarded the Victoria Cross. He is officially credited with 57 victories.

▷ aircraft – soon developed in Germany and France. Their eye-catching exploits offered hope that, even in the mechanised slaughter of the First World War, an individual could make a difference. The British did not publicise their aces, but by 1918 two British pilots had carved out great reputations among their peers: James 'Jimmy' McCudden and Edward 'Mick' Mannock.

Jimmy McCudden was an ordinary air mechanic when the war started, but all too soon witnessed a tragedy that would eerily presage his own death just four years later.

"We heard the engine stop and following that the awful crash, which once heard is never forgotten. I ran for half a mile and found the machine in a small copse of firs, so I got over the fence and pulled the wreckage away from the occupants, and found them both dead.

"I shall never forget that morning at about half past six: kneeling by poor Keith Barlow and looking at the rising sun, then again at poor Barlow and wondering if war was going to be like this always."

When McCudden got out to the Western Front, his keenness made him a natural to be taken up as an observer in the two-seater reconnaissance aircraft. Soon he was promoted to sergeant and had a memorable clash with the German ace Max Immelmann, flying the deadly Fokker Monoplane.

"The Fokker had by now turned and was coming towards our machine, nose on, slightly above. I stood up, with my Lewis gun to the shoulder, and fired as he passed over our right wing. He carried on flying in the opposite direction until he was lost to view. It was assumed that the Fokker pilot was most likely Immelmann. I was very thankful indeed to return from this outing. I had imagined that once Immelmann in his Fokker saw us, there was not much chance for us. However, we live and learn."

Highly strung

In July 1916, McCudden came home to learn to fly and qualified as a sergeant pilot, to be sent out flying DH2 scouts. He duly claimed five victories before returning to England as an instructor in February 1917. Among his pupils was Mick Mannock, who, at 28, was older than most pilots. An intelligent, highly strung individual, Mannock was torn by deep-seated fears and had great difficulty in scoring his first kill.

Right from the start, Mannock believed that air fighting was a science demanding relentless practice. Once he shot down his first German aircraft, he seemed to relax and was soon scoring on a regular basis. His success was based on diligent preparation, restraining caution, careful stalking and an understanding of the importance of pilots working together.

Lieutenant Ira Jones recalled Mannock's methods. "Suddenly his machine would rock violently, a signal that he was about to attack – but where were the enemy? His companions could not see them, although he was pointing in their direction. Another signal and his SE5 would dive to the attack. A quick half roll, and there beneath him would be the enemy formation flying serenely along – the result a complete surprise attack."

In all his teaching, Mannock was a great believer in one simple maxim: "Gentlemen, always above; seldom on the same level; never underneath." Altitude was vital in aerial fighting.

After McCudden's stint as a flying instructor, he returned to the fray as a flight commander, piloting the new SE5a scout with 56 Squadron in 1917. He was now the complete fighter pilot: his natural flying talents and accurate shooting were augmented by an absolute attention to detail when it came to checking his aircraft and guns. His professionalism was demonstrated in his pragmatic approach to the business of aerial warfare. He had no time for knight errantry.

"My system was to always attack the Hun at his disadvantage if possible, and if I were attacked at my disadvantage I usually broke off the combat, for in my opinion the Hun in the air must be beaten at his own game, which is cunning. I think that the correct way to wage war is to down as many as possible of the enemy

▲ A Royal Flying Corps squadron of fighter pilots proudly stand before their fleet of SE5 aircraft, the plane favoured by both McCudden and Mannock

▲ Mick Mannock relaxes on his final leave. By this stage he was buckling under the intense nervous strain of the aerial battles

at the least risk, expense and casualties to one's own side."

McCudden became an effective flight commander and his score mounted. As 1917 came to a close, both he and Mannock were approaching their peak. But 1918 would contain more air fighting than the rest of the First World War. Gradually swamped by the scale of the fighting, the great aces on both sides fell one by one.

In January and February, the mechanical skills that McCudden gained during his engine-fitter days added a whole new dimension to the menace he posed to high-flying German reconnaissance aircraft. He supercharged his SE5a scout to reach over 20,000 feet despite the intense cold and lack of oxygen.

"I saw a Hun LVG two-seater running away east, opened the throttle of the high compression Hispano and I overtook just as though he was going backwards. I quickly got into position and presented him with a very excellent burst from both guns, and he went down in a vertical nose dive, and then past vertical onto his back. The enemy gunner shot out of the machine, for all the world like a stone out of a catapult, and the unfortunate rascal seemed all arms and legs."

The spoils of war
Shortly afterwards, McCudden was again posted back home as an instructor. He was awarded the Victoria Cross and lionised by London society. Just four months later, he was promoted and sent out to command 60 Squadron in France. Flying out from England in his brand-new SE5a, he landed at the airfield of Auxi-le-Chateau to get directions. As his aircraft took off and banked, the engine stuttered and it crashed nose down into a nearby wood. Ground crew ran to the scene of the crash but found McCudden thrown out and lying beside one of the wings. He never regained consciousness and died the same day. One of the most deadly British aces of the war was dead, probably killed by a malfunctioning carburettor, his career stalled at 57 victories. He was just 23 years old.

Mick Mannock took McCudden's death very badly. By this time Mannock was a man coming to the end of his tether. He had always used humour to disguise his own jangling nerves, laughing away his fears, but in the course of this he developed a macabre mania for describing the consequences of being shot down in flames, as witnessed by Lieutenant Ira Jones:

"A swift tongue of flame followed by belching black smoke" – an illustration of the incident that claimed Mick Mannock's life

"Whenever he sends one down in flames he comes dancing into the mess, whooping and hallooing, 'Flamerinoes, boys! Sizzle, sizzle, wonk!' He describes the feelings of the poor old Hun, going into the minutest details. Having finished in a frenzy of fiendish glee, he will turn to one of us and say, laughing, 'That's what will happen to you on your next patrol, my lad!'"

His fears were such that he began to carry a loaded pistol in the cockpit in case his aircraft caught fire – there were no parachutes.

A highly strung individual, Mannock was torn by deep-seated fears and had great difficulty scoring his first kill

Mannock was evidently suffering from combat fatigue and he should really have been sent home. On his last leave, he had been more than usually moody, convinced he would be killed. A friend, Jim Eyles, reported physical reactions that clearly illustrated the strain the pilot was under.

"He started to tremble violently. This grew into a convulsive straining. He cried uncontrollably, muttering something that I could not make out. His face, when he lifted it, was a terrible sight. Saliva and tears were running down his face; he couldn't stop it. His collar and shirt front were soaked through. He smiled weakly at me when he saw me watching and tried to make light of it; he would not talk about it at all."

Yet his patriotic duty beckoned him still, and on his return from leave he was promoted to major and posted to take command of 85 Squadron. He at once began to hammer his men into a deadly fighting force, but he was taking more and more risks himself as his judgement deteriorated under the pressure.

Last patrol
Finally, on 26 July, Mick Mannock took Douglas Inglis, a young New Zealand pilot, up on a dawn patrol to try to get him a first victory.

"A quick turn and a dive," Inglis later recalled, "and there was Mick shooting up a Hun two-seater. He must have got the observer, as when he pulled up and I came in underneath him I didn't see the Hun shooting. I flushed the Hun's petrol tank and just missed ramming his tail as it came up when the Hun's nose dropped. Falling in behind Mick again, we did a couple of circles round the burning wreck."

From the ground, Private Edward Naulls saw the two aircraft flying low. "I watch fascinated as tracer bullets from a German machine gun post enter Mannock's engine just behind the cowling; there is a swift tongue of flame followed by belching black smoke and Mannock's machine falls away helplessly to hit the ground not far from his victim."

It all happened so quickly, but sure enough Mannock was dead – dying amid the very flames he had so feared. It was traditional for pilots to try and hold a defiant party, but Ira Jones found it a miserable affair.

"It was a difficult business. The thought of Mick's charred body not many miles away haunted us and dampened our spirits. There was more drinking than usual on these occasions; we tried to sing, but it was painfully obvious that it was forced."

Mannock has no known grave and the search to locate it still goes on. He would be awarded a posthumous VC in 1919. His final score was 73 victories.

Britain's two greatest aces and genuine working class heroes – Jimmy McCudden and Mick Mannock – were dead. They deserved recognition just as much as Richthofen, and after the war they were both much lauded. Their fame seemed for a while imperishable, but they are now forgotten heroes. We should remember them. **H**

Peter Hart is oral historian at the Imperial War Museum Sound Archive and the author of *Ace Falling: War Above The Trenches* (Phoenix, 2008)

••• PART THREE •••
THE STORY OF THE WAR

The war reaches an end, as **Peter Caddick-Adams** concludes his analysis of the 50 key elements that shaped the Great War

37 THE HOME FRONT

Prime Minister Lloyd George was one of the first to see that the home and overseas fronts were inter-related, observing, "We are fighting Germany, Austria and drink, and as far as I am concerned, the greatest of these foes is drink." Crowds of female munitions workers perhaps gave the greatest impression that social change was just around the corner.

After the introduction of conscription in March 1916, the government encouraged women to take the place of male employees. Whereas in July 1914, 212,000 women worked in engineering and munitions, by 1918 the total was nearly a million. The attractions were higher wages, better conditions and greater independence. Few would return to the poor wages and conditions of domestic service if they could possibly help it. The fact that some Home Front jobs were dangerous provided a further bond with men serving at the front. However, there were several spectacular explosions in munitions factories, and around 400 women died from overexposure to TNT whilst handling shells during the war.

One soldier remembered his embarrassment when bought a drink by a munitions worker; "You keep your money, Corporal. This is on us," he recalled. "She produced a roll of bank notes big enough to choke a cow. Many of the girls earned 10 times my pay as a full Corporal."

Bombing raids also had the effect of drawing everybody into the war. The raids, which killed 1,414 deaths, were a great social leveller, where all classes were equally at risk. As the conflict progressed, the nation's population and resources were harnessed to the war effort in one way or another, so most people came to feel involved.

Wearing a uniform of some kind (whether in the forces or as a male or female police officer, postal worker or bus conductor) was an obvious way of contributing, but civilians working in a factory making uniforms, guns, ammunition, tanks or ships had every right to feel they were contributing as much to the war effort as a man with a gun – as had dockers and miners and those working on the land.

▲ Bombing raids on London brought the war home to British civilians

ALAMY X2, GETTY

38 THE ADVENT OF RATIONING

Throughout the war Britain imported food by ship. To bring about surrender through starvation, the German Navy attempted to destroy these vessels using their submarine fleet. By the end of 1916, U-boats were sinking about 300,000 tons per month. In February 1917, they torpedoed 230 ships and the following month a record 507,001 tons of shipping was lost.

Initially, the government encouraged the population to voluntarily ration themselves, but this failed. Those who worked in factories did not get enough while anyone with money could buy on the black market. Food prices rose and by October 1916 coal was in short supply and rationed. Any area that could grow food was converted to allotments and livestock were kept in people's back gardens.

Malnutrition was seen returning to poor communities and the average weekly consumption of sugar and meat halved. Despite a policy of maximising food

production (the wheat harvest of 1917 was the highest ever recorded), some commodities, such as potatoes, were often in short-supply. In late 1917, fear spread that the nation was running out of food. Panic buying led to shortages and, in January 1918, the Ministry of Food decided to introduce ration cards and everyone had to register with a butcher and grocer. Rationing commenced with sugar, meat, butter, cheese and margarine.

The idea was to guarantee supplies, not to reduce consumption. This was successful and official figures show that the intake of calories almost kept up to the pre-war level.

Although unpopular, people had already got used to their freedoms being curtailed under the Defence of the Realm Act (DORA). Using this legislation, the government took over three million acres of farming land. From 1917, the Women's Land Army (WLA) and conscientious

▲ Lord Rhondda, Minister of Food, commandeers margarine in 1918

objectors replaced male agricultural labourers. Despite resistance, by the end of 1917 there were over 260,000 women working as farm labourers. The success of the WLA and rationing in 1917-18 contributed to its reappearance in 1939.

39 THE ROLE OF WOMEN

Active participation at the front was denied to British women throughout the war, but plucky individuals served with other nations. These included Flora Sandes in Serbia, and Mairi Chisholm and Elsie Knocker driving ambulances in Belgium.

Nursing became almost the only area of female contribution that involved being near the front and experiencing the war, though the War Office objected to any female presence in France or Belgium until 1915. Though later relaxed, the rules for joining the full-time Queen

Alexandra's Imperial Military Nursing Service (founded in 1902), in which over 10,000 served, stated personnel had to be single, over 25 years and of high social status.

With the part-time First Aid Nursing Yeomanry (FANY) and Voluntary Aid Detachment, founded in 1909 (with 41,000 nurses and orderlies by 1919), they tended the wounded in field hospitals, casualty clearing stations, aboard ambulance trains and hospital ships. The FANY also served in roles such as signallers, drivers, vehicle mechanics and dispatch riders.

The war brought new nursing challenges, such as coping with the effects of chlorine and mustard gas, shell shock and writing to the families of soldiers who died in their care. No prior training was provided for any of these. About 200 female nurses died on active service, mostly from air raids, whilst several were awarded Military Medals.

Late 1916 saw the Ministry of National Service establish female branches of the armed forces, designed to release men in noncombatant roles for the front. Some 57,000 served with the Women's Army Auxiliary Corps (later Queen Mary's Army Auxiliary Corps), founded in March 1917, and 5,000 with the Women's Royal Naval Service (WRNS). The Women's Royal Air Force (WRAF) was established on 1 April 1918, and attracted 9,000.

Over 3,000 Canadian women served during the war, alongside others from across the Empire – notably Australia, New Zealand, South Africa and India. More than 50 were lost at sea or died of disease. Culturally, taboos had been broken, and women in uniform were recognised as making an important contribution, respected and here to stay.

◀ Nurses in gas masks tend to the wounded in 1917

40 THE SPRING 1918 OFFENSIVES

Spring 1918 saw several major offensives against the Western Front, using German formations fresh from Russia. Collectively called the Kaiserschlacht, they were intended to punch through Allied lines, divide the French and British and force an armistice.

Though unrealistic, the strategy acknowledged that Germany was losing a war of attrition, with Ludendorff observing they must 'strike at the earliest moment before the Americans can throw strong forces into the scale. We must beat the British.'

Operation Michael, the main effort, hit the area between St Quentin and Amiens, where British defences were weakest, at 4.40 am on 21 March. The defending Fifth Army received 1.1 million shells in five hours, followed by stormtroopers, who overwhelmed forward positions. Within a day, the front was in shreds, signalling the end of trench warfare. This is the setting for R.C. Sherriff's play *Journey's End*.

However, Michael soon outstripped its logistics, running out of steam after three weeks. By April, the British had lost 255,000 to the Germans' 239,000, but on 26 March 1918, it prompted the long-overdue appointment of a Supreme Commander, the Frenchman Foch, to coordinate Allied strategy.

A second offensive, Georgette, developed on 9 April further north. Fearing a major catastrophe, Haig's 11 April Order of the Day concluded, 'With our backs to the wall and believing in the justice of our cause, each one of us must fight on to the end'. Logistics again intervened and Georgette had subsided by 29 April.

A third attack, Blücher-Yorck, attacked Allied positions further south on 27 May. Here, the Germans broke through as the local commander failed to study the new German methods. However, American troops blocked the Marne crossings at Château-Thierry, whilst US Marines defended Belleau Wood.

The Kaiserschlacht yielded huge territorial gains at the cost of depleting Germany's final reserves, including the elite stormtroopers. By July, the Allies possessed a quantitative superiority, increasing as more American troops arrived. German manpower was exhausted, and defeat became inevitable.

▶▶▶ 1918 – PAGE 96

▲ Exhausted American troops at the Rue du Pont (Bridge Road) at Château-Thierry, 1918

41 THE RAID ON ZEEBRUGGE

The plan to neutralise the key Belgian port of Zeebrugge, used by the German Navy as a base for submarines, sounds more like swashbuckling action from the Second World War than the First, dominated by its images of trenches and gas.

The raid was originally proposed by British First Sea Lord, Sir John Jellicoe, who argued it was vital to block the exits from Zeebrugge, as the U-boat menace had become so acute. Several obsolete vessels packed with concrete were to be sunk as blockships at the entrance to the Bruges Canal, whilst the elderly cruiser HMS *Vindictive* would land Royal Marines on the mile-long Zeebrugge mole to destroy the formidable shore batteries.

Led by Admiral Sir Roger Keyes and launched on the morning of St George's Day, 23 April, 1918, the operation began badly as the covering smokescreen was blown away revealing the raiding force to the coastal defences. *Vindictive* took a heavy pounding from the German gun emplacements and was unable to land her marines, who sustained heavy casualties, or use her main armament for fire support. The shore batteries disabled other blockships, the obsolete cruisers – *Thetis*, *Iphigenia* and *Intrepid* – and two converted Mersey ferries, the *Daffodil* and *Iris*, which scuttled themselves in poor positions, allowing the Germans passage to the canal. However, an old submarine, HMS *C.3*, did manage to blow up part of the mole.

An interesting case study in propaganda, both sides represented the Zeebrugge raid as a victory – the British exaggerated their success and awarded eight Victoria Crosses, though lost 200 killed and 300 wounded out of the 1,700 engaged – whilst the Germans boasted of their defeat of the raiders and returned the port to working order within days. Although not a runaway success, Zeebrugge, being preceded by RAF bombing raids, was in many ways the first tri-service maritime assault of modern times.

▲ British ships were scuttled in an attempt to block the entrance to the Bruges Canal

Dönitz developed the tactic of hunting in U-boat packs when attacking convoys

42 KARL DÖNITZ'S SUBMARINE WARFARE

Oberleutnant Karl Dönitz joined the U-boat arm from the surface fleet in 1916, becoming commander of the 500-ton UB-68, operating in the Mediterranean. By then, the Royal Navy had largely defeated the U-boat menace by introducing convoys, where merchant vessels, tankers or troopships sailed together as a group protected by naval escorts. It left U-boats unable to find easy lone targets, their prey of former years.

Dönitz and his friend, Wolfgang Steinbauer of UB-48, reasoned that if several U-boats attacked a convoy simultaneously, they could overwhelm the escorts, sink a few ships and escape. This was the basis of his Rudeltaktik (wolf pack) strategy, which he deployed in the Second World War. Both captains set out to put this idea to the test, but Steinbauer had to return with engine problems.

The 26-year-old Dönitz pressed on alone to ambush a convoy east of Malta on 3 October 1918. With his conning tower just above the waves, UB-68 penetrated the escort screen. As Dönitz said later, "On a dark night I met a British convoy, with cruisers and destroyers. I attacked and sank a ship. But the chance would have been very much greater if there had been a lot of submarines. That's the idea of a wolf pack, to put the submarines together, to attack together. From 1918 until 1935, when we had submarines again, I never forgot this idea."

Dönitz returned to find his convoy at dawn, but the UB-68 suddenly dived deep, out of control. Blowing his ballast tanks, Dönitz then shot to the surface, and emerged in full daylight to find he was in the middle of the convoy and under attack from the escorts Queensland and Snapdragon. With one crewman dead, the remaining 33, including Dönitz, surrendered. He was incarcerated first on Malta, then in a camp near Sheffield, where he fine-tuned the submarine tactics that he would use in the Second World War.

43 HOW THE COALITION WAGED WAR

The establishment of a Supreme Allied Commander, the French general Ferdinand Foch on 26 March 1918, illustrates a surprising aspect of the First World War. Although the range of nations on the Allied side (usually called the Entente) was extensive, there was little co-ordination of their activities.

Coalition warfare was not new – the campaigns of Marlborough, Napoleon and Wellington offered good prior examples that were studied in military schools – yet the advantages of formal co-operation and synchronising activities were never fully exploited.

The Austro-Hungarian assaults on Serbia and Montenegro made them natural Allies alongside the formerly neutral state of Belgium, occupied by German troops as part of the German Schlieffen Plan, with the original Entente powers – Britain, France and Russia. Japan (in 1914) and Italy (in 1915) joined subsequently and in 1916, Montenegro capitulated, leaving the

Entente, while two other nations joined – Portugal and Romania. The direction of the war changed on 6 April 1917, with the declaration of war by America. Russia left the alliance after the October Revolution, and the offensives of 1918 were principally conducted by Britain, France and America.

Coalitions are based on building trust between partners and, within Haig's BEF, two major colonial powers eventually came to prominence through their own expertise. The Australians and Canadians were eventually rewarded with their own army corps, each commanded by one of their countrymen, John Monash of Australia and the Canadian Arthur Currie, neither of whom were professional soldiers.

Foch's 1918 appointment, made in a moment of crisis during the German March offensive, marked a turn in the direction of the war. Yet it was a political move, brought about by national leaders concerned about the excessive casualty bills their countries were suffering. It would prove essential to

▲ Supreme Commander of the Allied Armies Ferdinand Foch oversaw the defeat of Germany

be able to coordinate the huge potential of America alongside the British and French forces. However, this still did not amount to coalition warfare as we understand it from 1939-45 or today. The armies fought essentially as national forces, with poor liaison, no interoperability and little understanding of each other's cultures.

44 THE CAVALRY ARE SENT IN

In 1914, all the major combatants used cavalry for reconnaissance, flank guards and shock action. From the Boer War, Britain – uniquely – trained its troopers as mounted infantry, able to operate in and out of the saddle.

War Horse reminds us how close all armies were to their horses in 1914, also relying on quadrupeds for artillery, logistical and medical support, at a time when mechanisation was in its infancy. Conditions for all equines were

severe at the front. They were killed by bullets and artillery fire, suffered from skin disorders, starvation and were injured by barbed wire and gas.

Trenches, barbed wire and machine guns all contributed to the cavalry's failure to provide a breakthrough on the Western Front, and some historians assert that by 1916 the horse had had its day, the tank was the future, and that the cavalry was only retained thanks to the patronage of men such as Haig, Allenby and Byng.

In some theatres, like the Eastern Front, Mesopotamia and especially Palestine, cavalry proved indispensable and, at Beersheba in 1917, a charge by the Australian and New Zealand Light Horse was instrumental in securing Allenby's victory. Yet, even on the Western Front, horses were deployed alongside tanks and aircraft, notably at Cambrai and Amiens, ready to exploit any breakthroughs that the slower tanks could not. New technologies and doctrine were still in their infancy, and armour was not in a position to replace the horse. True, larger bodies of horsemen were less effective, as the opportunities for their use were brief, but this was often the fault of the decision-making process, which was too inflexible and time-consuming to deploy them quickly.

There were moments when shock action worked, where lancer troops and squadrons were used in small-scale, combined arms attacks – in the 1918 Hundred Days Offensive horses, infantry and tanks operated together. Tactically, cavalry played a more important role than many historians have hitherto believed.

◀ English Light Cavalrymen keep watch for the enemy near Reims, 1914

US LIBRARY OF CONGRESS X2, SUPERSTOCK

Tragically, as many American troops died of influenza following the war as died in action

45 THE AMERICANS JOIN THE CAUSE

On the United States' entry into the war (6 April 1917), the Wilson administration and Congress realised that the Western Front would define victory, and the regular army and reserves of 125,000 would have to be expanded into a massive American Expeditionary Force (AEF). To accelerate deployment, they would use French and British weapons and equipment, and Congress pushed through a wartime conscription act in May 1918. Anticipation of this law drew many volunteers for the regular US Army, part-time National Guard and the national army of draftees.

Though the Air Service grew to 200,000, the main US contribution was on land, initially at St Mihiel, south of Verdun. Pershing (who had resisted attempts by the allies to feed his men into battle piecemeal under foreign command), assaulted on 12 September 1918, and his objectives were reached by the second afternoon. The Germans counter-attacked on 15-16th but were thereafter pushed back. St Mihiel resulted in fewer than 7,500 US casualties, an unprecedented 16,000 prisoners,

and was a great morale boost for Americans, justifying Pershing's 'American army' policy.

A second offensive, the Meuse-Argonne, followed immediately to break through the Hindenburg Line west of Verdun. Twenty-two US infantry divisions, only three of whom had previously seen action, six French divisions, plus tank support, totalling 500,000 men, attacked on 26 September in thick fog, but made slow progress. However, the flanks steamed ahead, led by Lt Col George S Patton's tank battalions, with Missouri artillery, commanded by future president Captain Harry S Truman. Positions were overrun, though Ludendorff soon counter-attacked. Pershing resumed the advance on 4 October and hard fighting continued until the 29th, when the Germans finally fell back.

Though hampered by poor staff work, logistics and doctrine, more than two million US troops reached Europe, including many after the Armistice. The AEF suffered 264,000 casualties, of whom 55,000 died in combat, plus the same again from the post-war influenza epidemic.

46 THE LAST HUNDRED DAYS

The Hundred Days was a sequence of land battles that defeated Germany on the Western Front, beginning on 8 August, and concluding with the November armistice. It succeeded the German Spring offensive, which breached the Allied lines, surged westwards, but had halted through exhaustion.

Foch and Haig decided to hit back and chose Amiens, where the Spring offensive had advanced furthest, but finally ebbed. At the junction of the British and French armies, allowing both to participate, the terrain was good "tank country" manned by weak German units.

In a single day of battle at Amiens on 8 August 1918, a vast hole was torn in the German lines. Achieving total surprise and numerical superiority, new allied tactics of infantry operating with artillery, tanks and aircraft gave Amiens a very modern 'feel', with the reward of 17,000 prisoners taken. Ludendorff called it 'the Black Day of the German Army'.

By 10 August, the Germans were pulling back to the safety of their Hindenburg Line, a web of concrete bunkers, trenches and barbed wire defences several miles deep. In the south, the French had also pushed the Germans back to the line, enabling Foch to plan a series of attacks all along its length.

The first blow of Foch's co-ordinated offensive fell on 26 September in the southern Meuse-Argonne area, using French and US troops. Two days later, British, French and Belgian soldiers attacked Ypres, to the north. On 29 September, British, Canadian and French forces hit the central St Quentin Canal defences. These successive hammer blows prevented Ludendorff from rushing reinforcements between threatened areas, but his army was already exhausted.

Accelerating moral and physical collapse eventually forced the German High Command to negotiate the armistice. Meanwhile, Allied pressure continued until the last minutes before the Armistice took effect on 11 November. A plaque in Casteau, near Mons, commemorates where the last shots were fired, just a stone's throw from where British and German cavalry first clashed in August 1914.

▲ Soldiers pass through the village of Hourges during the Battle of Amiens, August 1918

▲ The *San Francisco Examiner* celebrates the Armistice, which brought the First World War to an uneasy conclusion

47 THE ARMISTICE

Derived from the Latin *arma* (meaning weapons) and *stitium* (a stopping), an armistice is not a surrender or a truce, but a mutual agreement to cease fighting, as a mechanism to negotiate a lasting peace. There have been many armistices through history but that of 1918 is the most significant, giving rise to the observance of Armistice Day on 11 November in many countries.

It was inspired by President Woodrow Wilson's speech of 8 January, 1918, when Wilson outlined his war aims and hopes for the post-war world in Fourteen Points. Copies of the speech were widely distributed to boost morale at home, but also dropped behind German lines, to encourage a desire for peace.

Faced with a hopeless military situation, on 29 September 1918 the German Supreme Command recommended an immediate ceasefire and acceptance of Wilson's Fourteen Points, which were the only public statement of Allied war aims. German misgivings and Allied disagreement over using Wilson's ideas then caused a five-week delay. Entente statesmen had dismissed Wilson's speech as mere propaganda and had not foreseen it as the basis of any settlement.

Germany's position changed after the seamen's revolt of 29-30 October, when sailors, soldiers and workers began electing worker and soldier councils modelled on Russian soviets, advocating a range of freedoms, anti-military, political reforms and an end to the war. Faced with the proclamation of a republic, on 7 November a meeting was requested with the Supreme Allied commander. Crossing the front line, the German delegation was driven via the destroyed areas of Northern France to Foch's HQ train at Compiègne.

Over three days, the two sides discussed terms, amounting to a complete dismantlement of German war-making capability. With no negotiating room, the delegation finally signed at 5.00am on 11 November 1918. Hostilities ended six hours later. Technically, the Armistice lasted a month, but was extended twice for two further months, then for a year until peace was ratified at 4.15pm on 10 January 1920.

▶▶▶ THE 20-YEAR ARMISTICE – PAGE 116

48 SECOND WORLD WAR COMMANDERS IN THE GREAT WAR

Every senior officer of 1939-45 was a junior commander during 1914-18. Some were regulars, like Bernard Montgomery. Wounded early in 1914 as a platoon officer, once recovered he spent the rest of the war as a staff officer. By contrast, Bill Slim, also to rise to Field Marshal, had no intention of being a soldier, but joined the Territorial Army in 1914 and did well enough at Gallipoli and Mesopotamia to be offered a regular commission. Clement Attlee was another Gallipoli-Mesopotamia veteran, while Harold Alexander shone on the Western Front at Loos and Cambrai.

Bernard Freyberg emigrated to New Zealand aged two, but was a restless soul with no fixed career,

before being attracted to the war. Like some, he found he was simply rather good at soldiering, winning a VC. Charles de Gaulle, serving in the 33rd Regiment under Philippe Pétain, was wounded at Verdun and taken prisoner. Thereafter, he remained sceptical of the value of forts, like those at Verdun, or the later Maginot Line. Opposite him at Verdun was Friedrich Paulus, whose name became associated with another attritional bloodbath – Stalingrad.

Erwin Rommel was a pre-war officer, and spent most of his time at the front leading men, winning every decoration for bravery. He resented his year as a staff officer in 1918, though it probably preserved his life. Consequently, he never attended a

staff college, and emerged as a good battlefield tactician with ignorance of the higher levels of war. George Patton, an ambitious US cavalry officer, found himself commanding two battalions of tanks in September 1918. He was wounded, leading them on foot, but never forgot his appreciation of armour, or the exhilaration of being under fire.

Their experiences would govern the way they led in 1939-45 and colour their attitudes to friendships, subordinates, casualties, logistics and staffwork. The senior generals of the First World War had no such advantage, and though most British officers had some exposure to the Boer War (1899-1902), it was of a very different nature.

▲ 1940: Adolf Hitler decorates Erwin Rommel, who, like the Führer, had fought in the First World War

49 THE LITERATURE AND MEMOIRS OF THE WAR

Literature has played a huge role in interpreting the war, more so than with other conflicts. Initially, writers were buoyant, and respected figures like John Masefield, Rudyard Kipling, John Buchan and Arthur Conan Doyle lent their names to the war effort. The well-connected Cambridge graduate Rupert Brooke typified earlier war poets with his optimistic sonnet, beginning 'If I should die, think only this of me/ That there's some corner of a foreign field/That is for ever England'.

In 1915, Canadian doctor John McCrae left an unintended legacy with his mournful poem, 'In Flanders fields the poppies blow/ Between the crosses, row on row', composed in memory of a friend he had buried. His lines, about red poppies growing near Ypres, have since become associated with remembrance of the war.

Siegfried Sassoon was initially positive, but changed on witnessing the carnage. His work, with that of Wilfred Owen, perhaps best reflected the gritty realism of the trenches. They met when both were recovering from shell shock. Sassoon survived, but Owen's poetic legacy – *Dulce Et Decorum Est* and *Anthem for Doomed Youth* amongst the best-known – was always darker. Owen's impact is doubly poignant, for he was killed just days before the armistice.

C.E. Montague's *Disenchantment* appeared in 1922, an early prose work critical of the war, but most soldier-writers needed a decade before their literature appeared.

▲ Walter de la Mare makes a presentation to the celebrated war poet Siegfried Sassoon, in 1931

Edmund Blunden's *Undertones of War* and R.C. Sherriff's play *Journey's End* appeared in 1928. The biggest impact was made in 1929 by the German Erich Maria Remarque's *All Quiet on the Western Front*, a best-seller and successful film.

Robert Graves published *Goodbye To All That* in 1929, recording life in the same battalion as Siegfried Sassoon's *Memoirs of an Infantry Officer* (1930). Richard Aldington (*Death of A Hero*), American Ernest Hemingway (*A Farewell To Arms*) and Frederic Manning (*Her Privates We*) also published their literary responses to the war in 1929.

Most were written by former officers, but set the tone of critical memoirs for years to come

50 THE DEVELOPMENT OF BATTLEFIELD ARCHAEOLOGY

Recently, knowledge of 1914–18 has increased through battlefield archaeology. New methods have revolutionised the process of 'digging up the past'. Terrain can now be explored non-invasively, using technologies like ground-penetrating radar, and geophysical land surveys. Accurate mapping, enabled by GPS satellites, has allowed locations to be pinpointed with hitherto impossible accuracy, whilst metal detectors have allowed discarded, hidden or lost objects to be identified quickly.

Modern battlefields have become accepted as valid areas for traditional archaeology, television programmes have aided this and brought the discipline to wider attention, reflected by several university courses also on offer. Additionally,

forensic detection and analysis, routinely used by police forces and developed by the needs of the UN to respond to war crimes in Bosnia and Rwanda, means that human remains can now be identified, dated and sometimes even matched to specific individuals. In the context of 1914–18, with its huge numbers of 'missing' soldiers and the unidentified in cemeteries, the prospect of DNA testing probably means an end to future 'unknown warriors'.

In June 2001, French builders uncovered 20 British skeletons, buried with arms interlinked, and tentatively identified as members of the 10th Lincolns (the Grimsby Chums), lost on 9 April 1917, the first day of the Battle of Arras. They were reburied in a nearby war cemetery, but not identified further. By contrast,

a decade later, the Australian government had commissioned a huge archaeological dig at Fromelles, where 250 of their 'missing' soldiers were suspected to lie. Historians and forensics experts spent months uncovering artefacts and remains, identifying 120 of the 250 individuals.

As the last participants have died, we have only their written and recorded oral testimony of what life was like. However, archaeology offers additional evidence, rooted in fact, whereas the human mind is inaccurate and often confused in its recollections. As a result, past soldiers are better understood, for battlefield archaeology is not only identifying the dead, but recovering evidence of their day-to-day life. They will never be 'missing' in the same sense again.

▼ Modern scientific methods are illuminating the true story of the First World War

British soldiers take cover behind a barricade in Bailleul on 15 April 1918. The Germans took the town just a few hours after this picture was taken, yet their advance was soon to be repelled

MIRRORPIX

1918

FROM RETREAT TO VICTORY

Gary Sheffield charts the last year of the First World War on the Western Front, and reveals how the curiously forgotten victories of the Allies were based on military methods that led to the defeat of Germany

On the morning of 11 November 1918, Field Marshal Sir Douglas Haig allowed himself to savour the moment of victory. The fighting on the Western Front was, at long last, over. He was conferring with his senior commanders in Cambrai in northern France, a town that had been tantalisingly just beyond reach of the Allies for much of the war.

Haig was not given to populist gestures but, on the steps of the town hall, the winning team – Haig and his five Army commanders, plus the commander of the Cavalry Corps – were photographed for posterity. General Plumer, the commander of the Second Army, was instructed by Haig to "go off and be cinema'ed". Haig recorded that Plumer "went off most obediently and stood before the camera trying to look his best, while Byng (Third Army commander) and others near him were chaffing the old man and trying to make him laugh..."

It had been an amazing reversal of fortune. On 21 March, when the Germans smashed through the front of the British Fifth Army, the Allies had seemed on the verge of a catastrophe. But now Haig considered the news of the German defeat. He recalled "John Bunyan's remark on seeing a man on his way to be hanged, 'But for the Grace of God, John Bunyan would have been in that man's place'."

The battles that decided the First World War on the Western Front in 1918 were among the most significant in history. In March 1918, having defeated Russia, German high command sought to vanquish the British and French before the Americans arrived in sufficient numbers to make a significant contribution to the fighting. The German military leadership, Field Marshal Hindenburg and General Ludendorff, were well aware that this was a gamble for high stakes indeed. Victory would establish German hegemony in Europe,

The battles of 1918 on the Western Front were the largest that the British Army has ever fought

which would almost certainly have seen the extinction of liberal democracy on the continent and condemned millions of Europeans to a bleak future.

The battles of 1918 on the Western Front were also the largest the British Army has ever fought – and judging by the scale of the operations, the successful battles of the 'Hundred Days' from August to November 1918 constituted Britain's greatest ever victories. This was the only time in history when a British army, in a major European war, bore the brunt of fighting the main enemy in the main theatre of operations.

Curiously, however, the great battles of 1918 have little resonance with the British public today. Amiens does not have the same status as Waterloo or even Alamein. Instead, the bloody battles of 1916-17, the Somme and Passchendaele, are remembered for their huge casualties and alleged 'futility', the generals are labelled butchers and the soldiers are pitied as victims.

Tactical advances
A tactical revolution occurred during the First World War. This was partly because of the development of new weapons like gas and the tank, but more importantly, armies learned to use existing technology more effectively and incorporated it into an all-arms 'weapons system'.

In 1918, the Germans were first to take advantage of this. Employing effective tactics, achieving surprise and having a temporary advantage in numbers (192 German to 156 Allied divisions), on 21 March the Germans launched Operation Michael. The British Fifth Army, led by General Sir Hubert Gough, had only 12 infantry divisions, covering a 42-mile front in the Somme area, a consequence of Haig's (undoubtedly correct) decision to hold most of his troops in the north, covering the critical approaches to the Channel ports.

At 4.40am, German artillery opened up on British positions and, five hours later, waves of German stormtroopers attacked. Hampered by fog, inexperience in defensive fighting and, in some cases, low morale, the British ceded territory, 500 guns and 21,000 prisoners.

Yet the Germans were frustrated by stubborn resistance by parts of the Fifth Army, which prevented them from reaching all their objectives, while to the north the assault on Third Army made little headway. Over the next few days, Ludendorff was unable to convert tactical (battlefield) success into operational (campaign level) victory. He unwisely switched the main effort from place to place, dissipating the strength of his attack. In doing so, he failed to drive a wedge between the British and French, although the threat ▷

IMPERIAL WAR MUSEUM. ILLUSTRATION BY HANDMADEMAPS.COM

Sir Douglas Haig's 'winning team', pictured on 11 November 1918. Haig stands centre front

THE KEY OFFENSIVES OF 1918

Key
- – – Hindenburg Line
- ← German offensives Mar-Jul 1918
- ➤ limit of German advance
- ← Allied offensives Jul-Nov 1918
- OOO line at the Armistice 11th Nov. 1918
- 🜲 some major battles

1

Kaiserschlacht
The Kaiserschlacht (Imperial Battle), launched on 21 March 1918, broke through the front of the British Fifth Army and reopened mobile warfare.

2 Battle of the Lys
The Battle of the Lys began on 9 April 1918. Haig regarded this as the most dangerous German offensive, because it had the potential to threaten the Channel ports.

3 Second Battle of the Marne
Launched on 15 July 1918, the Second Battle of the Marne was the last major German offensive of the war, but was halted by the Allied counter-attack of 18 July 1918.

4 Offensive at Amiens
On 8 August 1918, the BEF's offensive at Amiens marked the beginning of the end of the war on the Western Front.

5 Meuse-Argonne
The battle in the Meuse-Argonne sector, which began on 26 September, was the largest US offensive of the war.

6 Breaking of the Hindenburg line
The breaking of the Hindenburg Line by the British Fourth Army on 29 September 1918 shattered Germany's last hope of stabilising the front in the west.

1918: from retreat to victory

German shock troops
prepare to go over
the top, March 1918

▷ that this might happen led the Allies to appoint Frenchman General Ferdinand Foch as overall Allied Commander, who sent his compatriots to aid the BEF.

Above all, the Germans failed to concentrate on capturing the critical communications and transport centres like Amiens, which, if lost by the British, might have crippled the BEF's ability to fight. In the end, Michael lost momentum and Ludendorff switched his attention north. Michael had created a bulge into the Allied lines some 40 miles deep that proved difficult to defend. The British had taken a battering, but were far from defeated.

On 9 April, Ludendorff tried again with Operation Georgette, a major attack south of Ypres. This was a graver menace than that posed by Operation Michael, as it threatened the Channel ports.

A Portuguese formation gave way, but on its flanks British troops fought on. As a consequence, the German advance of three and a half miles was confined to a narrow corridor. To the north, a 10 April attack wrested ground from the defenders – eventually the Passchendaele ridge, captured at a huge cost in lives only the year before, was abandoned. The situation seemed so serious that on 11 April Haig issued his famous 'Backs to the Wall' order.

A combination of stubborn British resistance and French reinforcements once again ensured that the Germans were unable to take advantage of their tactical successes. The cost was high. Between 21 March and 30 April, casualties amounted to 332,000 Allies and 348,000 Germans.

Ludendorff refused to give up, launching a number of

A proposed knockout blow in Flanders never materialised. The initiative had passed to the Allies

unsuccessful attempts to achieve that elusive decisive victory. What proved to be the final German offensive began on 15 July along the River Marne. Things went wrong from the start and, on 18 July, a major French-led Allied counter-offensive not only brought the German advance to a halt but also forced Ludendorff to face the reality of the destruction of his plans. A proposed knockout blow in Flanders never materialised. The strategic initiative had passed from the Germans to the Allies.

Why had Ludendorff's gamble failed? A couple of decades ago, there was a vogue for believing

that German tactics were hugely superior to those of the Allies. Many historians now argue that the German army developed tactics more or less in step with the British and the French, and that the use of 'stormtroopers' had some damaging side effects. First, it involved the concentration of the best troops in a few units, to the detriment of the rest. Second, once the stormtroopers had broken through the enemy lines, they kept advancing, but in doing so outran their own artillery – and infantry unsupported by guns had little chance of defeating a staunch enemy.

Since the German army lacked a mobile arm (the cavalry was mostly deployed on the Eastern Front and there were very few tanks), the Allies, although pushed back, were not routed. British and French forces were able to regroup, falling back on their sources of supply just at the point when German logistics started to fall apart. Add to this Ludendorff's defective generalship – especially his failure to maintain the objective and make all-out efforts to capture communication centres (not to mention the dogged fighting by soldiers from France, the USA and the British Empire) – and the result was a disaster for Germany.

Although large tracts of land were captured, they were ▷

CORBIS, GETTY X3

THE COMMANDERS

No-one shaped the momentous events of 1918 more than these three men

GENERAL ERICH LUDENDORFF (1865-1937)

Ludendorff bears a major share of the blame for Germany's defeat in 1918: for his lack of strategic judgement in launching the spring offensive in the first place and for his inept generalship from March to July. He successfully dodged the blame for the catastrophe that overtook the German army in the autumn of 1918, passing it on to the liberals and socialists who took over the wreck of imperial Germany – so fostering the notion of a 'stab in the back' that would later play into Hitler's hands.

DOUGLAS HAIG (1861-1928)

Haig is firmly associated with the bloody offensives of 1916-17 rather than the victory of 1918, and some historians see him as an 'accidental victor'. It is fairer to see him as taking a less 'hands-on' approach to command in 1918 than in earlier years – as a consequence of having experienced and capable subordinates – but nonetheless providing the overall vision and drive for the BEF. He was almost alone among the British in August 1918 in recognising that there was a real possibility of the war being won that very year.

FERDINAND FOCH (1851-1929)

Haig established a fruitful partnership with Foch as the Supreme Commander's principal lieutenant. He was an inspired choice: courageous, calm and mentally robust. The Grand Offensive was planned as a more modest endeavour, but he was convinced by Haig to broaden the scope. His authority was limited to that of a co-ordinator rather than a genuine commander but, by force of personality, he ensured the efforts of the Allied armies were meshed into an overall plan. Foch was indispensable to victory.

▷ to prove indefensible. The Germans suffered huge casualties, and the Allies were still in the fight. What is more, US troops were flooding into France, which undoubtedly depressed German morale.

The first fruits of the Allied capture of the initiative came at Amiens on 8 August. General Sir Henry Rawlinson's British Fourth Army, which consisted of British III Corps, the Canadian and Australian Corps, with French First Army in support, advanced eight miles in a day at a cost of 9,000 casualties (light by Western Front standards), inflicting losses of 27,000 on the Germans and capturing 400 guns. This success was of similar magnitude to 21 March but, unlike the earlier battle, Amiens was the prelude to success, not failure, with the Allies adopting a war-fighting philosophy strikingly at odds with Ludendorff's.

In 1917, the Allies had achieved a number of successes using 'bite and hold' methods: following heavy and concentrated artillery fire, infantry would advance to capture enemy positions, at which point they would halt, consolidate and wait for the guns to move forward and to begin the process again. At Hamel on 4 July, General Sir John Monash's Australian Corps used an updated version of these methods to capture all of its objectives in just 90 minutes – a model of a carefully prepared, tightly controlled set-piece battle with limited objectives. A pamphlet on the battle's lessons was circulated to the rest of the BEF. At Amiens, the Hamel methods were used on a far bigger scale.

The staff work and preparations for the battle were first rate and helped Rawlinson achieve complete surprise. Using a combination of deception and secrecy, the fresh and powerful Canadian Corps under General Sir Arthur Currie were brought to the Amiens area. A map captured during the battle showed that the Germans were totally unaware that Currie's men had left the northern sector of the front.

Element of surprise
Thanks to the advanced gunnery techniques that had been developed by this stage of the war, 2,000 Allied guns were able to fire without any preliminary bombardment – another crucial element in the maintenance of surprise. The number of guns and shells that were needed had been carefully calculated. Unlike in previous years, the BEF had an abundant superfluity of both: 700 field guns fired 350,000 shells. The counter-battery work of the heavy guns was highly effective, with most of the German guns neutralised, their crews either killed or driven off. Some 580 tanks were used. Infantry were in close support of the armour and 800 aircraft flew overhead to bomb and strafe the Germans.

The plan also called for reserve forces to follow on the heels of the initial waves. This was to allow them to pass through the assault troops once the first objective had been captured, to maintain the momentum of the attack. In all, Amiens demonstrated just how effective the BEF had become, integrating all combat elements, including airpower, into a battle-winning weapons system.

In his memoirs, Ludendorff called Amiens the "black day of the German Army". On 8 August, the Germans sustained a stunning defeat that marked the beginning of the end. The Allies had avoided Ludendorff's mistakes of the spring and, unlike the Germans, the BEF now possessed the guns and logistics to allow the point of attack to be switched quickly from sector to sector.

The key to success lay in fighting a series of limited operations, advancing seven or eight miles but breaking off the battle when the attack began to lose momentum, and then attacking elsewhere. The Germans were permanently on the back foot, constantly struggling to plug gaps in their defences. The

The Germans were permanently on the back foot, constantly trying to plug gaps in their defences

MIRRORPIX, GETTY

▲ An Allied soldier stands amid the rubble of Albert Cathedral, Picardy, during the German retreat of 1918

▲ A British Mark IV tank near Bapaume, 25 August 1918. Tanks were a key component in the Allies' new 'war-fighting philosophy'

BEF's infantry did not advance too far away from the safety of their artillery support, or outrun their lines of supply. This slow but steady operational method did not achieve the eye-catching advances that the Germans had managed in the spring, but it enabled Haig's forces to maintain steady pressure on the enemy, wearing down German strength and morale. Thus, following Amiens, the Third Army struck in late August across the 1916 Somme battlefield, while the French launched offensives to the south. By the end of September, the Germans had been hustled back to the Hindenburg Line, in the process abandoning the territory captured in the spring.

The Grand Offensive

Under Foch's direction, the Allied armies now launched a Grand Offensive: a co-ordinated, sequenced series of assaults along the entire front. First came the Franco-American attack on 26 September, in the Meuse-Argonne area. Then came the British First and Third Armies, attacking towards Cambrai on the 27th. Next was a push at Ypres on

28 September by French, Belgian and British divisions. The final act was the offensive of 29 September by the British Fourth and French First Armies. Here, the major breakthrough of the Hindenburg Line was achieved by a brigade of Staffordshire Territorials from 46th (North Midland) Division, which penetrated an immensely tough belt of defences including a portion of the St Quentin Canal.

The deeds of the elite troops of the Canadian and Australian Corps and the New Zealand Division have been rightly celebrated. The achievements of 46th Division reminds us that the contribution of British divisions should not be underrated. They were the bedrock of the BEF's victory.

Following the loss of the Hindenburg Line, Ludendorff stated that Germany faced "an unavoidable and conclusive defeat". He was correct. Although heavy fighting lay ahead, there was no way back for the German army and this led to the Armistice six weeks later.

At the last, there was a debate within Allied High Command about the terms that should be

accepted, or even as to whether the Allies should fight on. Various factors – suspicion among the Allies of each others' motives, fear that prolonged fighting might trigger a Bolshevik revolution in Germany, pessimistic intelligence reports – led to the adoption of Armistice terms that were severe but fell short of unconditional surrender.

German troops were able to return home rather than being taken prisoner. This had the unwelcome effect of helping many Germans, in the face of all the evidence, to persuade themselves that the German army had not been decisively defeated, which in turn led to the 'Stab in the Back' myth that benefited Adolf Hitler a decade later. In truth, the Allied armies were victorious and the terms of the Treaty of Versailles were a truer measure of the scale of the German military defeat. **H**

Gary Sheffield is Professor of War Studies at the University of Birmingham and the author of many books on the First World War

FURTHER READING

▶ *1918: A Very British Victory*
by Peter Hart (Weidenfeld & Nicolson, 2008)

HOW THE WAR WAS WON

The primary reason for the Allies' dramatic victory was their ability to win the tactical and technological war on the Western Front, argues **Jeremy Black**

In January 1918, many thought a German victory in the First World War possible. Defeat and revolution had left Russia tottering and, at Brest-Litovsk in March, the Bolsheviks accepted harsh German terms, allowing large numbers of German troops to transfer to the Western Front.

On 21 March, the Germans launched the first of their spring offensives, devastating the British Fifth Army on the Somme. That day, 21,000 British troops were captured and the British pushed back, leading Viscount Ebrington to note in May: "I am where I was in March and April 1915 – little did we think we should be here now."

Yet, six months later the Allies had won the war and Germany was suing for peace. How did this happen?

What explanations have traditionally been offered for the German defeat?

Allied victory has been explained in two different fashions. Some accounts focus on Allied forces out-fighting the German army on the Western Front. Others emphasise the German internal crisis created by the strains of the war, specifically the Allied blockade of the country.

The latter approach has tended to predominate, and the extent to which the Allies bettered the Germans militarily has not received the attention it deserves, including among the victors. The Germans, in particular, preferred the 'stab-in-the-back' legend, attributing defeat to left-wing disaffection at home, an argument later employed by the Nazis. Yet, in reality, the German forces in 1918 were defeated and dramatically driven back on the Western Front, in the very theatre where their strength was concentrated.

So, assuming that 1918 was very much a military victory, how were the Allies able to achieve this? Was it the impact of the Americans?

Between April and October 1918, over 1,600,000 American troops crossed the Atlantic, transforming a German superiority on the Western Front of 300,000 men in March 1918 to an Allied one of 200,000 men four months later. This was the largest movement of troops across an ocean to date.

The Americans were fresh and well fed, and, had the war continued longer, they would have made a crucial difference. The knowledge that they would be a factor certainly helped stiffen Allied resolve and influenced the German Supreme Army Command. From July, when they formed part of the effective French-commanded Marne counter-offensive, the Americans made a difference to the fighting.

What about developments in weaponry?

Artillery was very important. By 1918, Allied offensives were far more sophisticated than earlier in the war, featuring precise control of the infantry, massive artillery support, and better communications between the two.

With 440 heavy artillery batteries in November 1918, compared to six in 1914, the British army also had far more firepower to call upon. British gunnery inflicted considerable damage on German defences. The use of the creeping barrage (where artillery fire advanced slowly in front of the troops) had developed appreciably, as had counter-battery doctrine, science and tactics.

Aside from artillery-infantry co-ordination, the British had successfully developed planned indirect firepower. In contrast to direct fire (which relies on a direct line of sight between the weapon and its target), the use of indirect fire depended on accurate intelligence, including the extensive use of aerial photography as well as of sound ranging, surveying and meteorology. The use of artillery indirect fire has been seen as the birth of the modern style of warfare, in that it signalled the advent of three-dimensional conflict. Artillery certainly emerged as the key element in after-action reports in 1918.

How useful an innovation was the introduction of the tank for the Allies?

The British and French easily out-produced the Germans in tanks, and their availability contributed to a strong sense that the Germans had lost the advantage.

However, as was only to be expected of a weapon that had not had a long process of peacetime development, there were major problems with the reliability of tanks – and these were exacerbated by the shell-damaged terrain across which they had to operate. Many tanks broke down even before reaching the assault point, and in battle, tanks rapidly became unfit for service. They were not yet a fast-moving mechanised force.

Were there tactical improvements on the Allied side?

Technology was linked to tactics: more and better guns alone did not suffice. The tactical dimension was crucial, reflecting the long-term development of training, organisation and equipment that began for the British in 1915 and gathered

▲ Troops of the 803rd Pioneer Infantry Battalion on the USS *Philippine* off the French coast, July 1919

▲ German prisoners of war arrive in Southampton. As the Allies went on the offensive in autumn 1918, huge numbers surrendered

▲ British tanks advance, September 1918. Allied superiority in tank development showed that the Germans were losing the technology war

pace in 1916. The rapid infantry advance tactics that the British, like the Germans, employed in the latter stages of the war were linked to the development of more portable weapons, which could be carried forward by the infantry while still providing considerable firepower. Grenades, both thrown by hand and fired from rifles, were important, as were lightweight machine guns and mortars, and light artillery pieces.

The British also developed 'deep battle', a strategy in which they bombarded targets beyond the front, including reinforcements and headquarters. This development benefited greatly from aerial reconnaissance and air-ground support – all made possible by advanced and reliable aircraft, which were not available to the British before 1917.

Q How did the Allied military leadership contribute to victory?

A Command factors were significant to Allied success. There were certainly mistakes in planning and execution but, by 1918 – alongside improvements in the effectiveness of staff work at the General Headquarters and at corps headquarters – British commanders had greater relevant operational experience than in 1916. The adoption of unity of command under Ferdinand Foch in the last few months of the war also greatly helped the Allies.

Q How was Germany finally overcome?

A By late October 1918, not only had the Allies overcome the tactical problems of trench warfare, but they had also developed the mechanisms and deployed the resources necessary to sustain their advance.

The Allies broke through successive defence lines, significantly hitting German morale and undermining resilience and unit cohesion. As the Germans were pushed back onto the defensive, substantial numbers of troops either surrendered or deserted. On 26 October, German commander Ludendorff was dismissed. The German army had finally been beaten.

The Allies also defeated Germany's allies – Bulgaria, Turkey and Austria. The first to go was Bulgaria; its collapse showed how quickly an army could be defeated and a state could cave in. An Allied attack launched on 15 September on the Salonica front rapidly met with complete success. Allied troops were on Bulgarian soil within ten days, swiftly followed by a Bulgarian request for an armistice. The news led Ludendorff to also recommend an armistice. However, his decision was probably more affected by Allied successes on the Western Front than events in south-east Europe. ▣

Jeremy Black is the author of *The Great War And The Making Of The Modern World* (Continuum, 2011)

The day the guns fell silent

In 1918, at 11am on the 11th day of the 11th month, the fighting stopped on what many felt would be "the war to end all wars". **Malcolm Brown** tells the story of that most extraordinary day

GETTY

Joy on the frontline as troops
celebrate making it through the war

I t was a dull, dank morning. Weather-wise, it was going to be a typically lousy Monday. But this was a date with a twist in its tail. In Buckingham Palace that evening, Queen Mary wrote in her diary it was "the greatest day in the world's history".

One British soldier at the front took a similar view. Private Arthur Wrench of the Seaforth Highlanders wrote in his diary: "This day will be of great significance to generations to come. Surely this is the last war that will ever be between civilised nations."

Yet, from the moment it was announced, the news of the Armistice deeply divided opinion. In certain sectors of the Western Front, it produced dismay, even fury. For Captain Harry Siepmann, whose gun battery was relishing its hot pursuit of an enemy by now in full retreat, the instruction to cease firing arrived some time after 11am by way of a despatch rider on a motorcycle, who drove up noisily to their position and was bawled out for making such a din. Siepmann wrote: "It was not until he had gone that we opened the envelope and found that it did indeed contain the hated news. It was poor compensation to reflect that, in spite

of the Armistice, we had been in action at a few minutes to one o'clock on 11 November 1918."

A letter to his wife by Lieutenant Colonel Rowland Feilding, Commanding Officer of the 6th Connaught Rangers, explains why for some the news was so unwelcome. An advance was about to be launched that he claimed "would have been a bloodless victory, since the enemy was retreating so fast that it was difficult to keep pace with him." Thanks to the Armistice, it was aborted. "What a thousand pities that we have had to draw off at such a moment – just as we had the enemy cold."

More than a few voices would later regret that the chance to inflict an incontrovertible defeat on the German Army – or, indeed, go further and plant victorious Allied flags on German soil – had been thrown away by the decision to end hostilities.

The fear remains

But, for countless men in those parts of the front where the fighting was still fierce, close and personal, the predominant emotion on that final morning was not fury. It was fear. As the last hours ticked by, Sergeant Robert Cude noted in his diary: "If only I can last out the remainder of the time, and this is everyone's prayer. I am awfully sorry for those of our chaps who are killed this morning and there must be a decent few of them too." Cude was right. November 11th, like so many others, was to prove a bad day in the matter of casualties.

Yet, for those not in range of enemy guns, the countdown to 11am could be exhilarating. At 10.45am, artillery officer Lieutenant Arthur Gregory wrote: "My dear Mother: a quarter of an hour more war! This is my last letter on active service. Never again, I hope, shall I wear tin hat and box respirator. The church bells are ringing now. *Te deum laudamus* [we praise thee, God]."

Sergeant Arthur Vigars virtually chuckled his way through the appointed hour. In a letter to his fiancée, he wrote: "My dear Olive, hip hip. Another five mins and the war is nappoo – at least we hope so. 11.01am. Not even a parting shot from the artillery and so the war ends up in peace and quietness."

Quietness was not the order of the day on the outskirts of Mons in Belgium when the signalling officer of the 236th Canadian Regiment

1. The East Surrey Regiment salutes the news of the German surrender on 11 November 1918

2. British and American troops celebrate in Paris

3. Crowds gather to cheer the King and Queen at Buckingham Palace

BBC, CORBIS, GETTY, TOPFOTO

announced: "All hostilities will cease at 11 o'clock." The cheers the message raised brought out all the local people – including the sisters from a nearby convent – and in the twinkling of an eye, saucepans of coffee, wine, cognac, cakes, biscuits and apples appeared to provide the basis for a victory feast.

Convalescent camps and hospitals also joined in the celebrations. When Guardsman 'Fen' Noakes of the Coldstream Guards, recovering from his second wound of the year, was summoned on parade with his fellow patients that afternoon, they at once guessed the reason. The announcement made, they sang *God Save The King* and *Tipperary*, and when the Commanding Officer called for three cheers for the end of the war, Noakes remembered: "we almost cracked the clouds".

"Anyone that could run, walk or crawl went into the streets"

Artillery battery commander Major F J Rice reported a more muted reaction. His officers showed only modest enthusiasm at the news, though they did go so far as to visit a nearby anti-aircraft battery to buy a bottle of port. "We then went round the gun park and the harness sheds and told the NCOs and men. As an example of the calmness with which it was received, when we met Sergeant Goodall walking across the gun park and told him, he merely halted, saluted, said 'Very good, sir', and walked on!"

Quiet contemplation

One of the most poignant responses of the day came from the commander of the American Expeditionary Force's 315th Machine Gun Battalion, 80th Division, Major Leland Garrretson, in the region of the Argonne.

He wrote to his wife: "Peace at last reigns over this weary war-scarred land. Although all of us are of course ready to toss our hats in the air and howl with joy, under it all I believe most of us find ourselves thanking God over and over that this truly terrible thing is really and truly over. We all realise that our division is not an old campaigning division compared to the French and British veterans, but during the short time we were at it we were made to pay our precious toll and came to the thorough realisation that modern war is the most wholly awful thing ever conceived by the mind of man."

In Britain, the nation's capital became a focus of frenzied celebration. Shortly before 11am, the Prime Minister, David Lloyd George, emerged from 10 Downing Street and spoke to a boisterous, flag-waving crowd. "It is over," he said. "They have signed. The war is won!"

On the stroke of 11 o'clock, the all-clear was sounded from the plinth of Nelson's column ▷

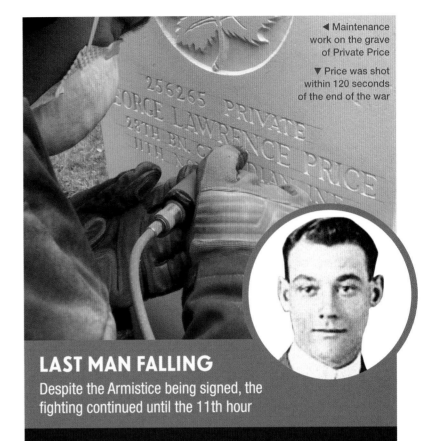

◀ Maintenance work on the grave of Private Price

▼ Price was shot within 120 seconds of the end of the war

LAST MAN FALLING
Despite the Armistice being signed, the fighting continued until the 11th hour

Certain soldiers acquired a tragic posthumous celebrity by dying a matter of minutes before the ceasefire on 11 November 1918. One such was 256265 Private George Lawrence Price of the 28th North West Battalion, 2nd Canadian Division, who lost his life at 10.58am in the small Belgian mining village of Ville-sur-Haine near Mons. There have been different views as to how he died. One version has it that he was killed during a final futile charge; another that he was one of a group of soldiers being thanked by local civilians for their recent liberation when a single shot rang out, killing him. Whichever was the case, his death so grieved his comrades that, 50 years later, survivors of the action returned to Ville-sur-Haine to unveil a bronze plaque in his memory, which is still preserved. Price is honoured in Canada and in Belgium, where a state-of-the art footbridge over a nearby canal is named after him.

The American Expeditionary Force can claim a final casualty even closer to time than Price. As 11am approached, Private Henry Gunther of the 313th (Baltimore's Own) Regiment was advancing with a crowd of other 'doughboys' (US infantrymen) on a German machine-gun position. Horrified, as they knew the war was about to end, the Germans waved the doughboys back, but Gunther kept advancing, was shot and died instantly. The time of his death was officially noted as 10.59am.

The last British fatality was L/12643 Private G E Ellison, 5th Royal Irish Lancers. Like Price, he died near Mons, when a dismounted patrol of the regiment was confronted by 20 well-entrenched Germans who fired and then fled. In this brief exchange, Ellison was shot and killed. His time of death was 9.30am. Both he and Price were buried in the military cemetery of St Symphorien, just a few miles east of Mons, originally built in 1914 by the Germans. By the strangest of coincidences, just yards away from Ellison's grave is that of the first British soldier to die in action on the Western Front, Private J Parr of the Middlesex Regiment. The date of Parr's death was 21 August 1914. The Private had been out on a scouting mission on a bicycle when he encountered some unfriendly Germans.

Hundreds of Londoners flocked to 10 Downing Street

FINAL DAY FATALITIES

The British and Empire servicemen who made the supreme sacrifice on Armistice Day died in no fewer than 36 countries. The records of the Commonwealth War Graves Commission – which lists all countries by their present-day names – show where they died:

France	278
UK*	243
Iraq	71
Iran	45
Belgium	29
Germany	26
Egypt, Greece and Russia (each)	18
Canada and India (each)	16
New Zealand	15
Israel	11
Ireland	9
Tanzania	7
Lebanese Republic and South Africa (each)	5
Italy	4
Ghana, Gibraltar, Kenya and Poland (each)	3
Belize, Mozambique, Namibia and Serbia (each)	2
Bulgaria, China, Malawi, Malta, Netherlands, Pakistan, Syria, Turkey, Yemen and Zimbabwe (each)	1
Australia	0
	Total: 864

*includes three women

GETTY X2

▷ in Trafalgar Square. In Winston Churchill's words, "the strict, war-stained, regulated streets of London became a triumphant pandemonium". Crowds thronged the approaches to Buckingham Palace and, when King George and Queen Mary appeared on the palace balcony, they were vociferously and repeatedly cheered.

One young officer who celebrated exuberantly that day was Lieutenant E D T 'Eddie' Edwardes who, while still officially a 'sick-case' recovering from being wounded in the field, was working at the Air Ministry on the Strand in London. He wrote to his mother: "As soon as the news was proclaimed, anyone that could run, walk or even crawl went into the streets, no-one did a stroke more work that day. When the guns and sirens commenced, Tyler and I went out to the Strand and the sight was quite hopelessly beyond description. Everyone went stark stamping mad. Tyler and I joined three WRAF [Women's Royal Air Force] girls (who incidentally were all 'igh-born lidies [sic]), bought flags, all got on to a motorcycle and sidecar and spent the whole day simply touring round and round London, cheering and yelling 'til practically speechless.

"Every time we stopped we gathered crowds and as soon as we'd got them nicely cheering, tore off to another street. We were photographed at Charing Cross and duly appeared next day on the back page of the Daily Sketch. Later we were joined by two other sick cases, went a party of six to a dance and didn't break off 'til seven in the morning."

Mixed emotions

When darkness fell, lights came on in the capital for the first time in many months. Bonfires and fireworks lit up the night sky. The theatres, restaurants, buses and tube were thronged with revellers. But there were those who could not celebrate. Notable among them was Colonel Alan Brooke, who had served in France with much distinction, and who, as Lord Alanbrooke, would become Britain's leading soldier in the next war. He later wrote: "That wild evening jarred on my feelings. I felt untold relief at the end being there at last, but was swamped with floods of memories of those years of struggle. I was full of gloom that evening, and retired to bed early."

Another recusant was the scholar, writer and future creator of Narnia, C S Lewis. 'Mafficking' was the standard term for celebrations after military success, ever since the famous raising of the siege of Mafeking back in the Boer War (1899-1902), and there was much evidence of that popular phenomenon that day. But this was anathema to Lewis who, in 1917, had studied at Oxford University with a group of young officers. Lewis wrote to his father: "The man who can give way to mafficking at such a time is more than indecent – he is mad. I remember five of us at Keble, and I am the only survivor. Let us be silent and thankful."

Meanwhile, across the Atlantic in New York, bells rang, whistles blew and cannons boomed.

▲ New York City erupts in ticker-tape on Armistice Day, 1918

"The strict, war-stained streets of London became a triumphant pandemonium"

Ticker-tape from the tops of buildings produced an avalanche of paper which, one report claimed, "littered the streets beneath almost to the extent of a foot in depth".

But nowhere was there more heartfelt relief than in France. "The French people are wild with joy," wrote American Medical Officer Major F J Sharp, in a letter written from Paris to his mother in Salt Lake City, Utah. "And one can hardly blame them, for they have suffered terribly. Two and a half million of her best men have paid the price of the supreme sacrifice." He added: "Many of our best have paid the extreme sacrifice but not like France in numbers. We will probably be friends with the French for ever."

So ended that most memorable of days. On that day, Private Wrench was far from being the only voice to express the belief that what had happened meant the end not just of the war thus concluded, but of the whole *concept* of war between the world's great nations. Prime Minister Lloyd George told Parliament: "Thus at 11 o'clock this morning came to an end the cruellest and most terrible war that has ever scourged mankind. I hope we may say that thus, this fateful morning, came to an end all wars."

At the front, artillery officer Lieutenant Colonel Bill Murray, who had fought in France ever since the early battles of 1915, wrote to his family: "No more danger. No more horrors. No more mud and misery. Just everlasting peace. It's a grand world." ⊞

Malcolm Brown has been a freelance historian attached to the Imperial War Museum in London since 1989

Watch an audio slideshow on the run-up to the end of the war at the BBC website ➨ bbc.in/PfjB8T

No more war

What awaited soldiers after the Armistice? **Peter Hart** reveals how those who survived the carnage coped with their mental and physical scars, and with the challenges of returning to a changed Britain

"The bloody war is over! It's over! And it was. No more slaughter, no more maiming, no more mud and blood, no more killing and disembowelling of horses and mules. No more of those hopeless dawns, with the rain chilling the spirits, no more crouching in inadequate dugouts scooped out of trench walls, no more dodging snipers' bullets, no more of that terrible shell fire. No more shovelling up of bits of men's bodies and dumping them into sandbags."
Lieutenant Richard Dixon,
Royal Field Artillery

These words echo the first reaction of most men when they heard the news of the Armistice on 11 November 1918. It seemed too good to be true. The Great

Repatriated British prisoners of war arrive at Hull, 23 November 1918. For thousands of soldiers, readapting to civilian life was far from easy

War had been a truly cataclysmic event. Vast empires had fallen and millions of men had died; millions more were crippled or maimed. The fighting had continued right up to the very last minute, but now it was suddenly all over.

Most men seem to have found it nigh on impossible to articulate the tangle of emotions that ran through their heads. Yet hard upon the feelings of freedom came the thoughts of what were they going to do now. Many had presumed that they would not live to see the end of the war. Part of their mental defence was the idea that they had nothing to look forward to; that as doomed men they did not have much to lose if they were killed. In a flash, their mental landscape had changed.

"An unreal thought was running through my mind. I had a future. It took some getting used to – this knowledge. There was a future ahead for me, something that I had not imagined for some years."
Lieutenant Richard Dixon,
Royal Field Artillery

The Armistice appeared to offer a wonderful template for a painless fairy-tale future where they could live happily ever after. But had things really changed? Many of the underlying pre-war problems had not disappeared with the defeat of Germany. There were still all the old international tensions, class warfare, looming economic disasters, racial hatreds and religious fanaticism to torment humanity.

But that was in the future. All most of the men serving in the British army wanted to do was to get out of khaki and safely back into their civilian lives as soon as possible. This, though, would prove to be a staggering administrative task. Millions of men would have to be returned to their former employments and if this was not controlled strictly, then economic chaos and mass unemployment loomed large.

Any demobilisation system had to be both transparently fair and carried out as soon as possible. Thus it was decided that men who were needed urgently at home to help re-stock the workforce of key industries would be released first, after which release would be grouped according to category and length of

service – with priority for those who had volunteered early in the war.

Among thousands of bored men, chafing under a now-redundant discipline, there were many disturbances, which could have been seen as mutiny if the bulk of officers and NCOs hadn't kept calm while a minority of hot-heads railed against the authorities. Guardsman Horace Calvert witnessed such an incident at Le Havre Camp in December 1918:

"I saw staff officers surrounded by a lot of troops and they were telling them they wanted money paid every week, they hadn't been paid for weeks; they wanted the right to go into Le Havre; they wanted the Military Police easing up a bit on them! The rumour was around that the last of the men to be called up would be the first to be demobilised...Chaps said they hadn't been home for four years and it was time they were allowed to go home. They were making a point and it was a forceful point...There was two or three hundred there. It wasn't a mutiny – I would call it a disturbance! They managed to disperse them eventually."
Guardsman Horace Calvert,
Second Grenadier Guards

It was not unnatural that men resented their continued service, especially as the army soon returned to its default state: a peacetime regime where 'spit and polish' ruled. But these men were not 'natural' soldiers. They had joined for the duration of the war and for no longer. The system may have been fair enough in principle, but it was inevitable that thousands of individual cases fell through the net. In the end, everyone seemed to have some reason or other to be dissatisfied within a demobilisation process that appeared to last forever.

"I was so useful in this camp orderly room, that the captain wouldn't sign my papers; he wouldn't let them go through. While other chaps were getting discharged I was still stuck in this blooming camp. One day I filled up my discharge papers and slipped them in amongst several others. The captain, who very rarely read anything – he just signed it – he signed my papers and two or three days ▷

Many had presumed that they would not live to see the end of the war. In a flash, their mental landscape had changed

▷ *later my discharge came through. He was furious!"*
Private Harold Boughton

Eventually they would all return home, free to try to pick up the elusive traces of their civilian lives. Too much was different: the world had changed while they were away. And they had changed. As thousands flooded the employment market, many men found it very difficult to get work.

"I applied for a job at Whitehall, at the Ministry of Labour as a temporary clerk. I went before a man, he was chairman and a lot of bearded old men round a board. The old men were in the saddle again and you just didn't stand a chance. He said, 'I'm sorry Mr Dixon, but you've had no experience!' Why, didn't I see red! I got up on my hind legs and said, 'Pardon me, sir! But I've had more experience than anybody in this room, but the thing is it's been the wrong sort! When I joined the army in 1914, I told the recruiting sergeant I couldn't ride a horse and he said, 'We'll bloody soon teach you!' They did and they spared no pains over it! Apparently I could be fitted for war but I can't be fitted for peace! I shall know what to do another time gentlemen!'"
Fred Dixon

Millions of men returned from the war to their homes, families and girlfriends. Most coped well, against all the odds managing to live reasonably contented lives. Yet many men found themselves alone in a crowd. No-one had really defined the nature of combat fatigue or post-traumatic stress disorder in the 1920s and little psychological help was available. Some soldiers back from the front had simply seen too much, experienced too many horrors, to go quietly into the tranquility of civilian life. The collation of symptoms known as shell shock was common, but barely commented on in public life.

"I think it sent me crackers a bit. One day the gaffer came, he said something to me and it just got right on top of me. I grabbed hold of him by the blinking lapel of his coat and I said, 'I'll split you top to bottom!' Stupid of me. I think he thought, 'Here's a crackpot come out from the war!'"
Albert Birtwhistle

A hidden world of suffering existed: a starched array of stiff upper lips, but with a dark unspoken undercurrent of men failing to cope with the pressures of civilian life and far too often resorting to casual violence. For many families, the Great War did not end in 1918 – thousands of women and children bore physical and mental scars that originated in the traumas of the battlefields.

Early plastic surgery
The badly wounded were the obvious victims. One such was Joseph Pickard, who had been smashed up by a shell on Easter Sunday 1918. He could never forget the loss of most of his nose. The evidence stared back at him every time he looked in the mirror.

"Can you ever imagine being without one? I never put the bandages back on; I got a piece of plastic to put across the hole...I didn't have any nose. All the kids in the blinking neighbourhood had gathered: talking, looking, gawping at you. I still had this little bit of plastic stuff as a nose. I could have taken the crutch and hit the whole lot of them! I knew what they were looking at. So I turned round and went back to the hospital. I was sitting one day and I thought, 'Well, it's no good, I can't stop like this for the rest of my life – I've got to face it sometime!' So I went out again – people staring – I used to turn round and look at them!"
Joseph Pickard

Some returning soldiers had simply seen too much, experienced too many horrors

In the end, Pickard underwent an early form of plastic surgery when, three years after the end of the war, a piece of his rib cartilage was used to rebuild his nose. It would never look quite right but it was a good deal better than nothing. There were many far worse off than him – and he knew it. William Towers had lost his leg in the war. Most people were sympathetic but there could be rank unpleasantness.

"He eyes me up and down, he said, 'I suppose you'll have to be living on other people's generosity for the rest of your life?' I said, 'Well it won't be your bloody generosity I want, goodbye!' And I walked away. I thought, 'Well I'll show that fellow if nobody else – I don't want their generosity!' Do you know it spurred me on!"
William Towers

Thousands suffered the phantom pains of missing limbs, the crippling disabilities, the callous jeers from children in the street, the irreparable rending wounds that reduced life to painful torture, wounds that cannot be looked at without a shudder of horror-filled empathy.

They inhabited a world of pain and suffering beyond comprehension: a world of tetraplegics, paraplegics, multiple amputations, wrecked lungs, mutilations, emasculation and blindness.

Perhaps in truth there could be no happy-ever-after for those returning from the Great War. This was no land fit for heroes. Not for the British people at any rate. The world economy had been severely over-strained and Britain found itself chained to an enormous national debt.

A worldwide depression left economies teetering on the brink of utter collapse. Once again it was ordinary individuals that suffered most in wave after wave of wage cuts, temporary lay-offs and redundancies.

Politics took a messianic turn with 'strong' leaders promising an end to all problems. Bubbling away in the background was the prospect of renewed conflict. The Great War was never really a war to end war – that was just a catchy slogan.

"We were told that this was 'the war to end war' and some of us at least believed it. It may sound extraordinarily naïve, but I think one had to believe it. All the mud, blood and bestiality only made sense on the assumption that it was the last time civilised man would ever have to suffer it. I could not believe that anyone who had been through it could ever allow it to happen again. I thought that the ordinary man on both sides would rise up as one and kick any politician in the teeth who even mentioned the possibility of war."
Lieutenant John Nettleton, Rifle Brigade

But, in reality, it was just another war. Bigger than any that had preceded it, perhaps, but, in essence, no different. Just 20 years later, the Great War would become the First World War with the onset of the Second World War. ∎

Peter Hart is the oral historian at the Imperial War Museum's Sound Archive. He is the author of *1918: A Very British Victory* (Phoenix, 2009)

1. British prisoners of war are given refreshments on a London railway platform on their arrival back in Britain, December 1918

2. A group of unemployed ex-servicemen carry a banner demanding work during the Great Railway Strike, September 1919

3. This 1918 illustration paints an idyllic picture of a soldier's return home to a rapturous welcome

4. A soldier is given first aid treatment, 1918. The wounded didn't always receive sympathy on their return home

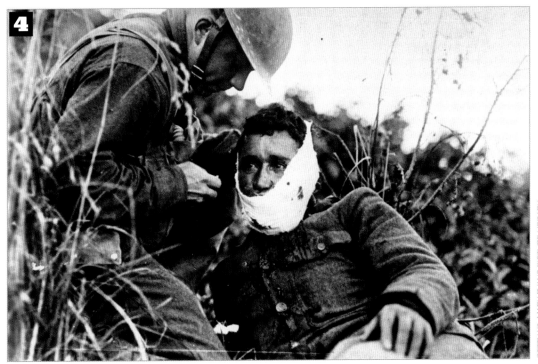

GETTY X3, MARY EVANS PICTURE LIBRARY

◄ Delegates assemble outside Foch's railway carriage in November 1918 where the Armistice was signed.

▼ In 1940, Hitler used the same railway carriage as the location for France's humiliation

The 20-Year Armistice

Historian **David Reynolds** explains to **Rob Attar** how the negotiations that ended the First World War came to have a lasting but disastrous legacy

Adolf Hitler was at the height of his power in June 1940 when he ordered Marshal Foch's former railway carriage to be removed from its museum and brought to a clearing in the French forest of Compiègne. The meaning was clear. Twenty-two years earlier, a German delegation had assembled in the Allied commander's carriage at this very spot to sign the punitive Armistice that ended the First World War.

This time, France – defeated by the Wehrmacht in a matter of weeks – was the country to be humbled. In the afternoon of 21 June, Hitler sat silently while the terms of a new Armistice were read out,

more severe in fact than those inflicted on Germany in 1918. But with its fighting capacity shattered, France had little choice but to accept. It was a moment of great symbolism for Hitler, summed up by his propaganda minister Joseph Goebbels: "The disgrace is now extinguished".

For a documentary on the First World War, historian David Reynolds visited Compiègne with director Russell Barnes and a film crew. The site of the two armistices was crucial to the film: how the closing of the First World War paved the way for the Second. "Historians are often interested in how wars begin," Reynolds says. "What I'm trying to show in

this film is that the way wars end are often as important, because here the seeds of future conflicts can be sown."

A harsh peace

The conditions the German delegation agreed to at 5am on 11 November 1918 were stringent. Germany was forced to abandon the territories it occupied, renounce its war gains and surrender much of its war-making machinery. "This armistice was a particularly harsh one," Reynolds explains. "The terms were reviled in Germany because they were obviously such a humiliation and didn't bear much of an obvious relationship to where the battle lines were when they

started to talk, at which point Germany was still deep into France and Belgium."

Yet the Germans felt they had no alternative but to accept the deal. Their army was overstretched and being pushed backwards. Meanwhile, Germany's coalition partners were either disintegrating or suing for peace. That September German commander General Ludendorff, already concerned about the failure of his earlier offensives, had panicked when Bulgaria sought terms, and declared his desire for an end to the war. As negotiations with the Allies got under way, the German position was further weakened by a collapse of the home front.

A sailors' revolt on 29 October sparked a revolution in Germany that was exacerbated by severe food shortages. With the country in turmoil, Germany's leadership needed a way out of the war, however bleak the consequences. "They were falling apart within," Reynolds explains. "Effective negotiation depends on a certain amount of equality at the bargaining table but the Germans had no way of resisting the pressure the Allies were putting upon them."

The burden of blame

However justified the German delegation may have been in signing the Armistice, the document still aroused great hostility in Germany. It would continue to do so for two decades. Although it had been the German military, and specifically Ludendorff, who had initially pressed for a cessation of hostilities, it was not they who were held culpable by the population at large. Critically, the revolution in Germany had ushered in a socialist-led democratic government that was at the helm when the Armistice was agreed and it

was this administration that the military sought to use as a scapegoat. According to Reynolds, the government was "blamed by the military for negotiating a humiliating armistice that it had not really had any great role in. The government got the blame for something that had been started by the High Command."

The resentment in Germany towards the Armistice endangered the postwar democratic Weimar government from the off.

An early warning of this was the assassination of the one civilian politician who actually signed the armistice, Matthias Erzberger, who was gunned down by a German nationalist in 1921. For the right wing in Germany, the Armistice was a convenient stick to beat both the democrats and socialists. The myth that they had been responsible for the Armistice was spread and exploited

> **"The Germans had no way of resisting the pressure the Allies were putting on them"**

particularly successfully by Nazi leader Adolf Hitler, who railed against the so-called 'November Criminals'.

Internal pressure

Despite having been the initiator of the Armistice, Ludendorff himself joined the charge and threw in his lot with the Nazis, even participating in the Munich Putsch of 1923.

The Weimar government attempted to shift the focus away from the First World War. However, when an economic collapse occurred in Germany in the early 1930s, it did not have the strength to take on the extremists. The 'betrayal' of 1918 aided the Nazis in their quest for power, a quest that would result in a brutal dictatorship and a second global war of arguably even greater savagery.

The Armistice damaged German democracy and helped precipitate another war. So were the Allies mistaken in imposing such

tough conditions on their foes? "When the negotiations were taking place," Reynolds explains, "it wasn't clear whether Germany would accept terms and it was only in the last few days that Germany fell apart. Allied commanders were fearful that Germany might decide to break off negotiations and resume the fighting. The imposition of the harsh terms of 11 November was motivated by the feeling that if everything went wrong and Germany started fighting again, the Allies wanted to have weakened its war-making powers as much as possible."

What the Armistice did achieve was a definite end to the First World War. That was the primary concern of the Allies, not the longer-term consequences. "People weren't looking that far ahead," Reynolds explains. "As with much of politics and political life you look to the next weeks and months. They weren't looking a year, let alone 20 years, down the line." ◼

David Reynolds has presented numerous history programmes on the BBC network.
Rob Attar is Editor of *BBC History Magazine*

BBC

THE ARMISTICE OF 1918
Paying the price for a war gone wrong

The terms offered to Germany in Marshal Foch's railway carriage were the result of negotiations – often heated – between Britain, France, the US and Italy. They stated that the Germans had to revoke their wartime gains, abandoning France, Belgium, Luxembourg and Alsace-Lorraine on the Western Front. In the east, Germany had to withdraw to its prewar borders, while the earlier Treaty of Brest-Litovsk with Russia was torn up. German soldiers also had to leave East Africa.

Germany's ability to start another war was severely reduced by the enforced surrender of war material, including 5,000 pieces of artillery, 25,000 machine guns and 1,700 aircraft. All German submarines were to be surrendered and several warships were to be disarmed and placed in neutral or Allied ports. Among the other conditions were the return of Allied POWs, the payment of reparations and the insistence that the Allied naval blockade of Germany would continue.

A German U-Boat in Britain following the end of the First World War. Germany had to give up all its submarines

Londoners observe a two-minutes silence at Piccadilly Circus on 11 November 1919. Remembrance Day 1919 was a sombre occasion, eschewing triumphalism

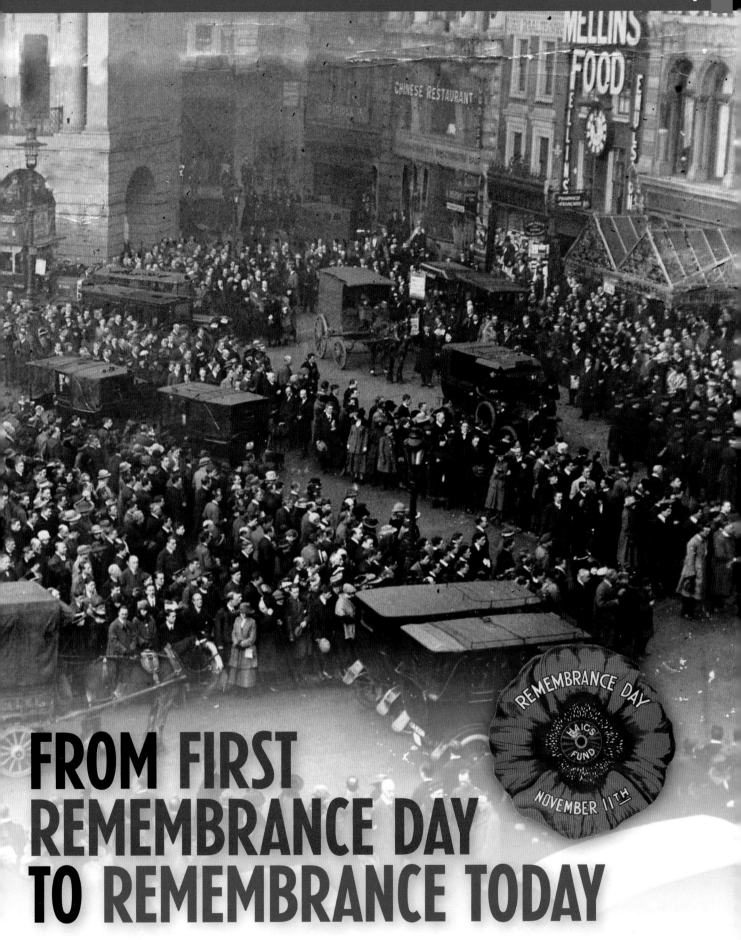

FROM FIRST REMEMBRANCE DAY TO REMEMBRANCE TODAY

In 1919, Britain first came to a standstill in honour of the dead of the First World War. **Fiona Reid** analyses how the way we commemorate the war has changed since that first Remembrance Day

The armistice of 11 November 1918 effectively ended the Great War – and many hoped that all wars had ended that day. However, the conflict was only officially concluded with the signing of the peace treaties in June 1919 and victory parades took place that summer. Yet some objected to exultant military parades, and a number of ex-servicemen even refused to participate. As a result, the first Remembrance Day ceremonies were commemorative rather than triumphant: "Today is Peace Day" announced the *Manchester Guardian* on 11 November 1919.

Two features of that first Remembrance Day are central to today's commemorations: the Cenotaph in Whitehall and the silence. Alongside

The minutiae of everyday life ceased completely in what *The Times* called "a great awful silence"

the official ceremonies, huge crowds gathered to lay wreaths at the newly erected Cenotaph. Many were wearing black, as at a funeral: this was a day of mourning, not celebration. The Cenotaph was the place around which people united – and the activity that united them was the two minutes of silence. On the King's initiative, people were asked to remain silent at 11am, to cease activity and stand with bowed heads, to think of the fallen.

To unite the whole country in a moment of contemplation required some organisation, especially given that times were not fully standardised throughout the UK. The silence was announced by maroons or church bells – and it was universally observed. Everything and everyone stopped: buses, trains and factories halted, electricity supplies were cut off to stop the trams and, wherever possible, even the ships of the Royal Navy were stopped. Workers in offices, hospitals, shops and banks stood still. Schools became silent. Court proceedings came to a standstill, as did the stock exchange.

Observing the silence

The minutiae of everyday life ceased completely in what *The Times* described as "a great awful silence". There had been no instructions about where people should observe the silence. It was assumed that everyone would simply pause at their tasks, but most chose to go outdoors to stand silently in a public place.

There were church services and the forces' chaplain spoke at the Cenotaph. However, Remembrance Day was largely secular. It was also a day for looking forward, and throughout the country thousands attended meetings in support of the League of Nations.

Other Remembrance Day traditions developed quickly. In November 1920, the 'Unknown Warrior' was buried in Westminster Abbey. The tomb contained the body of an unknown ordinary serviceman picked at random. It was laid in the

▼ London bus passengers pay their respects to the fallen. Everything from trams to Royal Navy ships came to a halt on the first Remembrance Day

REX X2

abbey in the morning and tens of thousands of people had walked past the grave by the end of the afternoon. Over a million people visited it in its first week.

The tomb was designed to honour the ordinary serviceman and to provide emotional or spiritual relief for survivors. The poppy campaign was more practical. From 1921, artificial poppies were sold to support the Earl Haig fund for ex-servicemen. Former soldiers made the poppies – and so ensured their own employment – and the profits supported ex-servicemen in need. Yet the poppy became symbolic too. Everyone wore one; in fact, it was soon so ubiquitous that its absence was the clue to solving Dorothy Sayers' 1928 murder-mystery, *The Unpleasantness At The Bellona Club*. The victim could not have died as claimed because no respectable fellow would have left the house without a Flanders poppy on 11 November.

There were other sides to Armistice Day. Postwar Britain was not a "land fit for heroes". It was a land of unemployment, poor housing and unrecognised pension claims. Some ex-servicemen grew tired of the perpetual homage to the dead veteran when surviving ones were receiving such little help. In 1921, disaffected former soldiers disturbed the commemorations at the Cenotaph.

And this was no one-off: unemployed ex-servicemen were to demonstrate at Remembrance Day ceremonies throughout the 1920s. The Ex-Officers' Association even began referring to Armistice Day as 'Obligation Day', when people had a 'Duty of Remembrance' to ex-servicemen in need.

Cause for celebration?

Conversely, Armistice Day also became associated with drinking, dancing and celebrating. Some argued that young people had been denied jollity for four long years. Why not let them celebrate? Yet, for others, it was too solemn an event for festivities and, in 1925, commemorative balls were cancelled. Ceremonies became increasingly sombre by the late 1920s and, in 1934, the Peace Pledge Union began to sell white poppies – overtly pacifist symbols – each November.

Local war memorials were erected throughout the 1920s. At annual ceremonies, the names of the dead were read out loud; the awful silence was now accompanied by a vocal acknowledgement.

Countless servicemen had died without family funerals and 100,000 of them had no marked grave, so local memorials functioned as both familial and national sites of mourning. People also visited these sites on the days that were crucial to their own war. 11 November was not the most significant day for everybody: survivors remembered the day they first went over the top, the day their best friend died, or the last time they saw their husband.

Remembrance Day events were scaled down during the Second World War. The 1918 victory seemed hollow and people had to think about the current war, not the previous one. After

1945, both conflicts were remembered on the Sunday closest to 11 November. This signified a real change in the nature of the ceremony. In the interwar years, a poignant two-minute silence had annually been inserted into the fabric of an ordinary day. After the Second World War, those who chose to commemorate the wars went to some sort of service (usually in church) each year. The commemorations were thus marginalised. For the postwar generation, they meant little.

Yet, by the 1990s, as veteran numbers declined, there was a growing public interest in the Great War, and there was a modern-day resurgence of the 1930s disillusionment literature, notably Sebastian Faulks' *Birdsong* (published in 1993) and Pat Barker's *Regeneration* (from 1991). Meanwhile, there was a political decision to restore the two-minute silence in 1996: once again it was to become an integral part of national life.

In 2008, three British First World War veterans attended the commemorations at the Cenotaph on Remembrance Day. The following year there were none. That war is still meaningful – thousands attended the funeral of last-serving First World War veteran Harry Patch in August 2009 – but the meaning of Remembrance Day has changed, despite a determination to maintain the outward symbols.

So what is the purpose of today's ceremony? With British troops still engaged overseas, Remembrance Day can seem like a glorification of war, as an inducement to further sacrifice: it is clearly a military ceremony. Alternatively, is 11 November a day for pacifist sentiment? Should we still call it 'Peace Day'? Certainly Harry Patch's popularity lay partially in his willingness to condemn all war as futile.

Remembrance Day has never been a homogeneous, nationally unifying event. It has provoked a variety of responses over the last 90+ years: triumphalism, reverence, anger, pacifism, celebration. And no doubt it will continue to do so. Perhaps we should take this annual opportunity to think seriously about wars and their consequences. ⓗ

▲ Last man standing: Harry Patch was the last First World War veteran to die. He passed away in July 2009

Fiona Reid is the author of *Broken Men: Shell Shock, Treatment And Recovery In Britain 1914–30* (Continuum, 2010)

On the Armistice Trail

Following in the footsteps of those who fought in the final week of the Great War, **Paul Reed** visits locations that played a key role in the countdown to Armistice

The last seven days of the First World War saw British and Commonwealth forces pursuing a retreating enemy between the towns of Le Cateau and Mons in northern France and Belgium. Ironically, it was the same ground over which the army had fired its first shots in 1914. The Armistice Trail allows you to visit in one day some of the key locations connected with the war's final week – where the last shots were fired and where the last men fell.

1 Lock No 1

The final great battle of the First World War took place on 4 November 1918 with the crossing of the Sambre Canal and the rupture of the last line of German defence in northern France. This was not trench warfare; it was open combat more reminiscent of Normandy than the Somme. On the extreme right flank of the British advance was Lock No 1, a small canal lock that offered a narrow but easy crossing for men of the Second Royal Sussex Regiment, supported by Royal Engineers and Australian Engineers. Crossing open ground, the meagre barbed wire defences were dealt with by engineers of both nations, albeit under fire from the Lock House.

Three Australians died here – the last of the war to fall. Reaching the canal, the Sussex men crossed under point blank machine-gun fire. Today, a small memorial records the Sussex sacrifice. Both Lock and Lock House are the originals that stood here in 1918.

2 Ors cemetery / Wilfred Owen

Wilfred Edward Salter Owen is arguably one of the seminal voices of the First World War. The poet served on the Somme and Hindenburg Line, before being evacuated home with

▲ Ors cemetery, home to Wilfred Owen's grave. The celebrated war poet was killed just seven days before the end of the war

shell shock. Returning to the front in 1918, he was awarded a Military Cross for capturing a machine-gun post. He was killed on 4 November while his battalion, the Second Manchesters, were attempting to cross the Sambre Canal near to the village of Ors. The telegram announcing his death arrived one week later, just as the church bells were signalling the Armistice.

Ors today is proud of its connection with Owen: there is a memorial near the canal and Owen is buried in the communal cemetery. He shares a plot with two VC heroes of the same action: Jimmy Kirk of his own battalion and James Marshall of the Irish Guards.

3 La Capelle

As the German nation plunged into civil unrest fuelled by starvation, the Kaiser abdicated and Chancellor Paul Von Hindenburg telegrammed Marshal Foch to call for negotiations for an end to the war. On 7 November 1918, a group of German parliamentarians crossed the French lines at 8.20pm, near to the village of La Capelle. The party met troops of the French 171st Regiment and were safely conducted to Tergnier, where they went by train to Compiègne and met Foch to sign the Armistice. A memorial to commemorate this historic event was erected at the site in November 1925, but was completely destroyed by the Germans following the Fall of France in 1940. Rebuilt in 1948, it proudly proclaims, in French, "... here triumphed the tenacity of the Poilu [French infantrymen]".

▲ An Englishman, Irishman, Welshman and Scotsman lie side-by-side at Nouvelles

4 Nouvelles Communal Cemetery

While St Symphorien cemetery is a popular pilgrimage for those wishing to see the graves of the last few to die in the war, this small communal cemetery is arguably just as important. There are only nine burials here, one of which is unknown. But in two rows are the two ends of the war: the grave of Captain Dawes, who died in August 1914 during the Battle of Mons, and just a few feet away four men who died on

Lock No 1 pictured today ▲ and during ▶ the First World War. The last three Australians to lose their lives in the war fell here

PAUL REED X5

The arched entrance of Mons town hall commemorates those Allied soldiers who fell nearby

11 November 1918 while serving with the Royal Naval Division.

Incredibly, these burials represent the United Kingdom: there is an Englishman, Irishman, Scotsman and Welshman. Two were volunteers, two conscripts. One, Harold Walpole, had been wounded three times; the last was to kill him. More than any other location on the Armistice Trail, this site presents a significant snapshot of the men who served in those final days of war.

5 Mons Town Hall

Canadian troops, under the command of Sir Arthur Currie, reached the outskirts of Mons on 10 November 1918. By this stage, the news of the forthcoming Armistice had reached senior commanders. However, Currie thought it would be significant if the war ended at the place where it had started four years before and, on the night of 10 November, launched an attack into Mons. The following morning, two veteran Canadian battalions – the Princess Patricia's and Royal Canadian Regiment – had a 'race' to the main square and town hall, reaching both as the war came to an end.

In the archway entrance to the town hall, memorials commemorate the liberation and the Fifth Lancers who fought nearby. The visitor's book (livre d'or), which Currie and many officers signed, can be viewed on application to the mayor's office.

6 Mons Museum

This important collection of First World War artefacts opened in the 1920s, with the museum focusing on the fighting at Mons in 1914 and the closing days of the war when the Canadians arrived. Aside from the usual array of uniforms, weapons and equipment, there are some unique pieces. Among them is the original headstone from George Lawrence Price's grave. He was originally buried in a communal cemetery at Havre and had a grave made from local stone.

7 Price Memorial

George Lawrence Price is accepted by the Commonwealth War Graves Commission to be the last British and Commonwealth soldier to die in the Great War.

On the last morning, his battalion despatched patrols along the roads leading northeast beyond Mons. In Ville-sur-Haine, they came under machine-gun fire from the opposite side of the Mons-Conde canal which ran across their axis of advance. It's believed that Price was among those sent to investigate and, after crossing a canal bridge, reached a street of terraced houses. No gun was found, but while chatting with Belgian civilians, thanking the Canadians for liberating the area, a single shot rang out and Price fell wounded. He was dragged into a nearby house, where he died at 10.58am.

In 1968, surviving comrades erected a plaque on the house where Price died, but the house was demolished when the canal was widened in the 1990s. The plaque now stands on a plinth close to where Price fell.

8 St Symphorien

Not only is St Symphorien arguably the most tranquil of all the First World War battlefields, it is unique in many ways; not just in the rare contrast between the British and German burials, but the fact that the first and last casualties are buried here. John Parr fell at Mons while on patrol work on 21 August 1914. He was just 16. Directly opposite – and more by accident than design – lies the last British Army casualty, George Ellison. In France since 1914, he served

▲ The grave of George Ellison, the last British soldier to die in the First World War, at St Symphorien cemetery near Mons

right through to the last day, falling 90 minutes before the end, as his cavalry regiment, Fifth Lancers, advanced beyond Mons.

Only a few feet separate Parr and Ellison, but between them are the million dead of Britain and the Commonwealth, along with four years of bitter conflict. ∎

Paul Reed is a military historian and broadcaster who has worked as a consultant on several BBC TV programmes about the First World War

1923

A series of tough post-war treaties imposed upon the defeated Central Powers radically re-drew the map of Europe. The Habsburg Empire was dismantled in a major way; Austria and Hungary became separate states, Romania expanded, and the new states of Czechoslovakia, Yugoslavia and Poland were created.

Poland also consisted of land from the Russian Empire, now replaced by the USSR. The Baltic states of Estonia, Latvia and Lithuania were also established.

Germany lost Alsace-Lorraine and Northern Schleswig to France and Denmark respectively, while the new Polish Corridor separated Germany from its enclave East Prussia.

NORWAY

NORTH SEA

DENMARK

IRISH FREE STATE

Dublin

UNITED KINGDOM OF GREAT BRITAIN & NORTHERN IRELAND

London

NETHERL.

Hamburg

Brussels

BELGIUM

LUX.

GERMANY

Paris

ATLANTIC OCEAN

Bay of Biscay

FRANCE

SWITZ.

Munich

PORTUGAL

SPAIN

Madrid

Lisbon

ITALY

Rome

FURTHER READING

The literature on the First World War is both volumnous and heavily detailed. Here are some suggestions for digging a little deeper...

GENERAL

A Military Atlas Of The First World War
Arthur Banks
(Pen & Sword, republished 2001)

The Great War
Correlli Barnett
(BBC Books, republished 2003)

The Sleepwalkers: How Europe Went To War In 1914
Christopher Clark
(Allen Lane, 2012)

The Quick And The Dead: Fallen Soldiers And Their Families In The Great War
Richard van Emden
(Bloomsbury, 2011)

The Soldier's War: The Great War Through Veterans' Eyes
Richard van Emden
(Bloomsbury, 2009)

The Beauty And The Sorrow: An Intimate History Of The First World War
Peter Englund
(Profile, 2011)

Almost a century on, the First World War fallen continue to be remembered at memorials across Europe and beyond

The Routledge Atlas Of The First World War
Martin Gilbert
(Routledge, republished 2008)

To End All Wars: How The First World War Divided Britain
Adam Hochschild
(Macmillan, 2011)

The First World War: A Very Short Introduction
Michael Howard
(Oxford University Press, 2007)

Six Weeks: The Short And Gallant Life Of The British Officer In The First World War
John Lewis-Stempel
(Weidenfeld & Nicolson, 2010)

The Great War: An Imperial History
John Morrow
(Routledge, 2003)

Broken Men: Shell Shock, Treatment And Recovery In Britain 1914-30
Fiona Reid
(Continuum, 2010)

Home Before The Leaves Fall: A New History Of The German Invasion Of 1914
Ian Senior
(Osprey, 2012)

Forgotten Victory: The First World War – Myths And Realities
Gary Sheffield
(Headline, 2002)

The Chief: Douglas Haig And The British Army
Gary Sheffield
(Aurum Press, 2011)

Hide and seek: from behind barbed wire, a French soldier tracks German troops on the Western Front in 1915

The Confusion Of Command: The Memoirs Of Lieutenant-General Sir Thomas D'Oyly 'Snowball' Snow 1914-1918
Dan Snow & Mark Pottle
(Frontline, 2011)

1914-1918: The History Of The First World War
David Stevenson
(Penguin, 2004)

The First World War
Hew Strachan
(Simon & Schuster, 2003)

The First World War In Africa
Hew Strachan
(Oxford University Press, 2004)

Artillery In The Great War
Paul Strong & Sanders Marble
(Pen & Sword, 2011)

BATTLES

 The Somme: The Untold Story In Never-Before-Seen Panoramas
Peter Barton
(Constable, 2011)

 Passchendaele 1917: The Story Of The Fallen And Tyne Cot Cemetery
Franky Bostyn & Jan van der Fraenen
(Pen & Sword, 2007)

 Gallipoli
L A Carlyon
(Bantam, 2011)

 Flanders 1915: Rare Photographs From Wartime Archives
Jon Cooksey
(Pen & Sword, 2005)

 Battle Story: Gallipoli 1915
Peter Doyle
(The History Press, 2011)

 Battle Story: Loos 1915
Peter Doyle
(The History Press, 2012)

 Gallipoli: The Ottoman Campaign
Edward J Erickson
(Pen & Sword, 2010)

 Somme: The Heroism And Horror Of War
Martin Gilbert
(John Murray, 2007)

 Aces Falling: War Above The Trenches
Peter Hart
(Phoenix, 2008)

 Gallipoli
Peter Hart
(Profile, 2011)

 The Somme
Peter Hart
(Phoenix, 2006)

 The Western Front
Richard Holmes
(BBC Books, 1999)

 The First Day On The Somme: July 1 1916
Martin Middlebrook
(Penguin, 2006)

 Bloody Victory: The Sacrifice On The Somme
William Philpott
(Abacus, 2010)

 The Somme
Robin Prior & Trevor Wilson
(Yale University Press, 2005)

 The Somme
Gary Sheffield
(Cassell, 2003)

 Command And Control Of The Western Front: The British Army's Experience 1914-18
Gary Sheffield & Dan Todman (eds)
(The History Press, 2007)

 The German Army At Passchendaele
Jack Sheldon
(Pen & Sword, 2007)

 The German Army At Ypres 1914
Jack Sheldon
(Pen & Sword, 2010)

 The German Army On The Western Front 1915
Jack Sheldon
(Pen & Sword, 2012)

 Jutland 1916: Death In The Grey Wastes
Nigel Steel & Peter Hart
(Phoenix, 2004)

 They Shall Not Pass: The French Army On The Western Front 1914-1918
Ian Sumner
(Pen & Sword, 2012)

VICTORY, ARMISTICE AND AFTERMATH

 A Shattered Peace: Versailles 1919 And The Price We Pay Today
David A Andelman
(John Wiley, 2007)

 The Great War And The Making Of The Modern World
Jeremy Black
(Continuum, 2011)

 1918: A Very British Victory
Peter Hart
(Weidenfeld & Nicolson, 2008)

 Peacemakers: Six Months That Changed The World: The Paris Peace Conference Of 1919 And Its Attempt To End War
Margaret Macmillan
(John Murray, 2003)

 11th Month, 11th Day, 11th Hour: Armistice Day 1918, World War I And Its Violent Climax
Joseph E Perisco
(Random House, 2004)

 Summits: Six Meetings That Shaped The 20th Century
David Reynolds
(Penguin, 2008)

 With Our Backs To The Wall: Victory And Defeat In 1918
David Stevenson
(Allen Lane, 2011)

 How The War Was Won: Factors That Led To Victory In World War One
Tim Travers
(Pen & Sword, 2005)

 Remembering War: The Great War And Historical Memory
Jay Winter
(Yale University Press, 2006)

▶▶▶ And also, to keep up with the latest First World War research and discoveries, why not take out a subscription to *BBC History Magazine*?
www.historyextra.com

"THE BELIEF THAT THE WAR WAS NECESSARY HAS BEEN FORGOTTEN"

The vast number of First World War casualties prompts us to ponder the futility of war. But, as **Hew Strachan** points out, the cause for which they fell is often neglected

Over the next few years, particularly between 2014 and 2018, we are going to stand before our local war memorials, looking at the names of those who went forth to the Somme and Passchendaele, to Gallipoli and Mesopotamia, and who did not come back. Quite a few of us will travel to see the graves, still so beautifully tended by the Commonwealth War Graves Commission. We may be moved to tears, by the youth of those killed or by the words put at their relatives' request on their headstones. And too many of us may repeat those accusatory adjectives thrown so often at the First World War: 'wasteful' and 'futile'.

There is a paradox here. How can we honour those who died if we do not honour the cause for which they gave their lives? The question is still pressing today, as we struggle to differentiate between our support for the armed forces (which is high) and our doubts about the wars in which they are engaged (for which we blame not them but politicians).

Today's soldiers rarely describe their deeds as patriotic or ideological, preferring instead to stress professionalism and comradeship. However, those who fought in the First World War were mostly citizen soldiers, whose values reflected the society from which they were recruited.

Last letters home may not be particularly reliable sources for the way soldiers felt. They were composed by men who knew that they would have to provide succour to their families in their despair, so they were not going to use words like 'wasteful' or 'futile'. Equally, they could not afford to tell lies in these, their final words to their loved ones. We too quickly pass over their references to the justness of the cause. If we treat those beliefs flippantly, we cannot in

Few of those who died doubted the legitimacy of what they were doing

truth be honouring their authors or their motivations.

Remarkably, few of those who died doubted the legitimacy of what they were doing. Of course, they could not afford to, given that they were sacrificing their own lives for it. Nor could those who mourned believe anything else, because to accept that their deaths had been in vain would be both a betrayal of their memory and an end to one form of consolation.

But this belief that the war was both necessary and in a good cause, that it was – in the words inscribed on the Victory Medal struck by Britain after the war ended – "the Great War for civilisation", has been largely forgotten.

In 1904, Britain and France came to an understanding that formed part of the reason why the British army went to Europe ten years later. The entente required Germany to see it as a hostile alliance for it to become one. It was a resolution of outstanding colonial disputes between two imperial powers, a continuation of old diplomacy between two great powers, more than it was a harbinger of the war that ushered in the modern world. But the *Manchester Guardian*, whose editor C P Scott would oppose Britain's entry to the war in July 1914, welcomed "the new friendship" for "the chance it affords of a genuine alliance between the democracies in both countries for the furtherance of a common democratic cause".

We need to reintegrate these ideas – which suggest that the First World War was fought for values that we also respect – as we approach its centenary. If we cannot admit competing and sometimes contradictory interpretations of the war, then its commemoration is unlikely to deepen our understanding, and so will prove as futile and wasteful as the stock clichés about its appalling losses. ⬚

Hew Strachan is Chichele Professor of the History of War at the University of Oxford

▼ Cemeteries, like this one at Verdun, will be the focus of public contemplation as the war's centenary approaches